Generating internationally comparable
income distribution estimates

Generating international compar-
uing the scrub than estimates

Generating internationally comparable income distribution estimates

Edited by Wouter van Ginneken and
Jong-goo Park

International Labour Office   Geneva

ACKNOWLEDGEMENTS

Work on this project took place between 1980 and 1983. We would like to thank, first of all, Helen Hughes and Felix Paukert, who are - so to speak - the founding parents of this project and who have encouraged us all along. In the World Bank, it was originally Bhanoji Rao who started working on it with much enthusiasm. We would further like to thank all collaborating authors who were patient enough to bear up with our probing comments. Finally, we had much benefit from the comments of Felix Paukert, Gerry Rodgers and Rolph van der Hooven on the before-last draft of this monograph.

Wouter van Ginneken
(ILO, Geneva)

J.-G. Park
(World Bank, Washington, DC)

CONTENTS

I. METHODOLOGY AND RESULTS

The question of income distribution became a matter of major importance in the last United Nations Development Decade. This is explained by the fact that not all groups in society benefited equally from economic growth and that in some developing countries the absolute number of poor has not decreased. As a result, various attempts were made to produce a set of internationally comparable income distribution data. Given the fragility of underlying data, most of these attempts have been criticised.[1] The attempt described in this monograph, which is the result of collaboration between the ILO and the World Bank, represents a new effort to improve international comparability - an effort that, it may be hoped, will be followed by further improvements in the future.

The collection of income distribution started with the efforts of Adelman and Morris,[2] who included 43 distributions from developing countries, with different income concepts and income units. Their work was supplemented by Paukert,[3] who achieved better comparability for 56 developed and developing countries, since he chose primary income as the income concept and the household or the family as the income unit. The collection of income distribution data was further extended by S. Jain,[4] who included information on 83 developed and developing countries (often more than one distribution per country). The collection contains distributions with different income concepts, income units and geographical coverage. M. Sawyer[5] produced comparable pre-tax and post-tax income distribution data on a per household and a per head basis for about 12 OECD countries. P. Visaria[6] reviewed the income distribution data of six Asian countries (or regions) and experimented in particular with various income units (households, household member and equivalent unit) and their impact on income distribution and poverty analysis. O. Altimir[7] produced comparable income distribution data for seven Latin American countries. He used the same methodology for adjusting various income sources for inconsistency with National Accounts. The income unit he employed is the household while the income concept is total household income (including primary income, property income received, current transfers and other benefits received minus employers' contributions to social security). C. Morrisson[8] generated a series of income distribution data, including 40 developing countries. The income concept employed is primary income while the income unit is household, person or income earner. Income data are in some cases adjusted for inconsistency with National Accounts. Finally, the United Nations Statistical Office[9] produced a new compilation of income distribution data. Each of the 60 country chapters contains information on concepts, sample design and sampling errors, as well as on tabulations undertaken and selected actual results.

The 23 income distribution estimates included in this monograph are based in principle on the same income concepts and income units (see section 1). Moreover, the original survey data have been adjusted, where necessary, for inconsistency with population estimates and National Accounts (see section 2). Section 3 presents the results of the estimates; it shows the per household distributions as well as the per head distributions (for 14 countries). Finally, for a few countries it was also possible to estimate per head and the per equivalent unit distribution (see section 4). In this introduction we shall also deal with the question of grouped data and ranking problems (see section 5). Lastly (in section 6), we should like to give some suggestions for further research.

1. Income concept, income unit
    and recipient unit

The income concept employed in the project is total available household income as defined by the United Nations Provisional Guide-lines.[10] It includes wages and salaries in cash and in kind (excluding social security and private insurance contributions both by employers and employees), net income from self-employment (including consumption of own produce), income from personal property and investment (including imputed rent of owner-occupied housing), social security and private (insurance) transfers, minus personal income and property taxes. This type of definition covers only part of total welfare, i.e. "that part of total welfare which is attributable to the consumption of goods and services of the kinds which are normally sold on the market".[11] In other words, welfare derived from government services and from having children is not included in this definition.

The income unit which corresponds with our income concept is undoubtedly the household. The household concept adopted here will be as close as possible to the definition of the 1980 World Population Census Programme:[12]

> A household may be either (a) a one-person household (...), or (b) a multi-person household, that is, a group of two or more persons who make common provision for food or other essentials for living.

Most previous studies analyse the distribution of households by household income. Although the household is the central unit within which production and consumption decisions are taken, it is not sure whether it is an appropriate recipient unit. If one wishes to analyse the primary income distribution, it seems that the income earner or tax unit is more appropriate. Depending on the aim of the analysis, one could also defend using the household if one is interested in the earning power of a household. It is, however, not completely consistent to consider the household as the recipient unit for available household income (i.e. income after tax and transfers).   The reason is that households of different size and composition need a different amount of available income to reach the same level of economic welfare.

As a result, more and more authors are proposing to look at the distribution of persons by household income per head.   Danziger and Taussig,[13] for example, claim that the person is a more appropriate income-receiving unit than the household.   This is confirmed by Sen,[14] who states that - for poverty analysis[15] - the person is the appropriate unit because, from a social welfare point of view, one should weigh each individual's welfare equally.

If one can derive equivalent scales (indicating the relative income needs for persons of different age and sex) it is clear that household income per equivalent unit is a better criterion of economic welfare than household income or household income per head.   One would therefore come to the conclusion that the distribution of persons according to household income per equivalent unit is the best way of looking at the distribution of economic welfare.   For eight countries we were able to estimate the equivalent scales using a methodology which is explained in section 3.   However, there is a small problem with the distribution of persons according to household income per equivalent unit in that it does not fulfil the so-called "aggregation criterion".

If one looks at the distribution of households by household income and of persons by household income per head, the aggregated income is equal to total income in the population.   The third distribution consistent with the aggregation criterion is the distribution of equivalent units by household income per equivalent unit.   However, we do not consider this distribution appropriate since the number of equivalent units is not the correct welfare unit. As Sen points out,[16] the adoption of this unit would imply that the economic welfare of three two-member households would get a higher weight than two three-member households.[17]

In figure 1 we show the nine combinations of recipient units and income measures (ranking criterion).   It shows that of the nine possible distributions, the distribution in cell 6 is considered optimal, those in cells 1 and 5 are sub-optimal, while those in the other cells are considered unimportant.

It is likely that the distribution of persons by household income per head is fairly close to the optimal distribution.   This is so because they have the same receipient unit (the person) and because - as we shall see in section 4 - the equivalent scale factor is closer to one than to zero.

Figure 1: The nine combinations of recipient units and income measures

Recipient unit (weighting criterion)	Income measure (ranking criterion)	Income per household	Household income per head	Household income per equivalent unit
Household		1	2	3
Person		4	5	6
Equivalent unit		7	8	9

2. Consistency with National Accounts and population estimates

In most cases, income distribution data are derived from household income and/or expenditure surveys and are, therefore, based on a sample. As a result, the quality of the data on incomes and households is dependent on sampling and non-sampling errors of those surveys. There is not really a theory about how income and population data should be adjusted. In this monograph we shall therefore take a pragmatic approach. There are basically two facts which make an adjustment necessary. First, in many surveys small households tend to be under-represented, while the number of large households is over-represented. As a result, the per head and per equivalent unit distributions are biased. It is relatively straightforward to correct for this bias if a reliable estimate of the household size distribution is available. In a number of case studies, this adjustment was made - normally based upon population census data. The second basic fact is that aggregated income - as measured by household surveys - underestimates National Accounts income by between 15 and 30 per cent. It can generally be assumed that National Accounts data are more accurate than aggregate household income estimates, because the former data combine multiple data sources and have been subject to several rounds of consistency checking. In some countries, however, outcomes of income and expenditure surveys have been used to "construct" the National Accounts totals.

Table 1: Gini-indices and decile distributions (in percentages) - adjusted available income per household

		I	II	III	IV	V	VI	VII	VIII	IX	X	Gini-index	Deviation from the standard income concept[1]
Bangladesh	1973-74	2.7	4.1	5.1	6.3	7.6	8.5	10.2	13.3	14.8	27.4	0.35	(BT)
Denmark	1976	2.9	4.5	5.6	7.0	8.5	9.8	11.3	12.9	15.1	22.4	0.30	(-IR)
Egypt	1974	2.1	3.7	4.9	5.8	6.8	7.9	9.5	11.3	14.9	33.2	0.40	-
Fiji	1977	1.1	2.6	4.0	4.8	6.0	7.4	9.4	11.5	15.5	37.8	0.47	(BT)
France	1975	1.8	3.5	4.9	6.2	7.4	8.6	10.0	11.8	15.3	30.5	0.39	(-IR)
Germany (Fed. Rep.)	1974	2.9	4.0	5.0	6.0	7.1	8.3	9.9	12.0	16.0	28.8	0.37	(-IR)
India*	1975-76	2.5	3.4	4.5	5.8	6.4	7.5	9.0	11.5	15.8	33.6	0.42	(BT)
Islamic Rep. of Iran	1973-74	1.4	2.4	3.3	4.2	5.6	6.5	8.3	10.9	15.8	41.7	0.52	-
Ireland	1973	2.5	4.7	5.3	7.8	8.2	8.4	10.4	13.3	14.3	25.1	0.32	(-IR)
Kenya	1976	0.9	1.8	2.6	3.7	4.9	6.6	8.9	10.3	14.6	45.8	0.59	-
Mexico	1968	0.7	2.0	2.8	3.6	4.5	5.7	7.5	10.6	15.9	46.7	0.56	-
Nepal*	1976-77	1.8	2.8	3.4	4.6	5.2	6.5	7.5	9.0	12.7	46.5	0.53	(BT)
Panama	1976	0.7	1.3	2.0	3.2	4.7	6.3	8.4	11.6	17.6	44.2	0.57	(BT)
Philippines*	1970-71	1.9	2.6	4.1	4.9	5.8	6.9	8.5	10.5	15.3	38.8	0.46	(BT)
Sierra Leone*	1967-69	2.0	3.6	4.5	5.1	5.8	6.9	8.8	10.8	14.7	37.8	0.44	(BT)
Spain	1973-74	1.9	3.8	5.1	6.5	6.9	8.9	10.2	12.7	16.0	28.0	0.37	-
Sudan*	1967-68	1.2	2.8	4.0	5.0	6.5	8.5	10.0	12.5	14.9	34.6	0.44	(BT)
Sweden	1979	2.6	4.6	6.1	6.7	7.5	9.9	11.8	13.6	16.0	21.2	0.30	-
Tanzania	1969	2.1	3.7	4.9	5.3	6.4	7.5	8.9	10.8	14.8	35.6	0.42	-
Trinidad and Tobago*	1975-76	1.6	2.6	3.8	5.3	6.5	7.4	9.5	13.3	18.2	31.8	0.45	-
United Kingdom	1979	2.8	4.5	5.5	6.9	8.2	9.5	10.9	12.5	15.5	23.8	0.32	-
Yugoslavia	1978	2.4	4.2	5.4	6.7	8.2	9.4	11.6	13.4	15.8	22.9	0.33	(BT)
Zambia	1976	1.0	2.4	2.9	4.5	5.2	6.0	7.6	9.3	14.8	46.3	0.56	-

1 BT = before tax; -IR = not including imputed rent.
* Partially adjusted to National Accounts.

Table 2: Gini-indices and decile distribution (in percentages) - adjusted available income per head

		I	II	III	IV	V	VI	VII	VIII	IX	X	Gini-index	Deviation from the standard income concept[1]
Bangladesh	1973-74	3.6	5.2	6.4	7.2	8.5	9.4	10.2	11.7	14.4	23.4	0.28	(BT)
Denmark	1976	4.0	5.5	6.4	7.3	8.2	9.0	10.4	12.2	14.7	22.3	0.27	(-IR)
Egypt	1974-75	2.8	4.8	5.1	5.9	6.7	7.5	9.4	10.7	13.9	33.3	0.38	-
Fiji	1977	1.4	2.8	3.9	5.4	6.0	7.3	8.8	11.1	15.3	38.0	0.46	(BT)
France	1975	3.2	4.7	5.3	6.0	6.9	8.2	9.5	11.9	16.0	28.2	0.35	(-IR)
Germany (Fed. Rep.)	1974	3.6	4.8	5.7	6.7	7.4	8.7	9.9	11.6	14.8	26.8	0.32	(-IR)
India*	1975-76											0.38	(BT)
Islamic Rep. of Iran	1973-74	2.3	3.3	4.1	4.9	5.8	6.9	8.3	10.8	14.9	38.8	0.47	-
Ireland	1973	3.5	5.5	6.2	6.5	8.1	9.4	10.2	10.9	14.8	24.9	0.29	(-IR)
Kenya	1976	0.8	1.7	2.6	3.6	4.8	6.4	8.7	10.1	16.4	45.0	0.59	-
Mexico	1968	0.7	1.9	2.6	3.5	4.4	5.7	7.4	9.9	15.5	48.5	0.58	-
Spain	1973-74	2.6	4.6	5.5	6.2	7.6	9.1	10.5	12.2	15.4	26.4	0.34	-
Sweden	1979	3.5	6.0	7.1	8.3	9.1	10.1	11.4	12.4	13.5	18.5	0.22	-
United Kingdom	1979	3.9	5.6	6.3	7.2	8.0	9.1	10.5	12.0	14.8	22.6	0.27	-

1 BT = before tax; -IR = exceeding imputed rent.

* Partially adjusted for National Accounts.

There are many reasons for this discrepancy. After a thorough survey of Latin American data, Altimir[18] comes to the conclusion that "biases in sample structure and in responses to income questions appear to be less important sources of discrepancies than underestimation of income". He further finds that[19] "estimates of property income (housing in particular) are higher in surveys than in the National Accounts, which tend to undervalue this item. Survey figures for wages and salaries are in most cases consistent with National Accounts total (...). Entrepreneurial income in the survey data is usually 25-50 per cent below the comparative macro-economic estimates." It seems, therefore, necessary to adjust survey data in order to provide a more realistic picture of income inequality and in particular of the incomes received by high income classes. It is the adjustment of profit and capital income which tends to increase measured inequality.

Many authors have proposed ways to make these adjustments. Ojha and Bhatt[20] and Ranadive[21] proposed to take the expenditure distribution and to estimate separately savings ratios per expenditure class. The rationale of this methodology is that expenditure gives a more accurate picture of the economic welfare (in particular of low income groups) because expenditure in kind is normally valued at retail prices and because expenditure is usually more closely related to permanent income. This approach was followed in several case studies (such as Egypt, Islamic Republic of Iran, and Tanzania and Yugoslavia). Mrs. de Navarrete[22] proposed a similar methodology for Mexico but she adjusted the incomes of higher income groups somewhat differently. In fact, for all income classes where measured income exceeds measured expenditure, incomes were proportionally increased in order to arrive at consistency with National Accounts. For income classes where measured expenditure exceeds measured income, expenditure is taken as a proxy for income.[23] Part of this procedure was used for the Philippines and Trinidad and Tobago. Altimir proposes to adjust the original household income distribution by type of income. In other words, he corrects separately wages and salaries, income from self-employment, property income and transfers for inconsistencies with National Accounts. This methodology was followed in various countries, such as Denmark, Fiji, France, Ireland, Mexico, Spain, Sweden and the United Kingdom. The three methodologies normally lead to a higher estimate of income inequality, but to a lower estimate of poverty.

There is in principle, however, no limit to the number of adjustments that can be made. If a social accounting matrix[24] is available, the original survey data have been made consistent with various sources of data, such as population estimates, data from tax and social security surveys, population and industrial censuses.[25] This type of adjustment was applied for the Federal Republic of Germany, Kenya and Zambia. The most advanced way of adjusting is a so-called merge-file,[26] which, on the basis of various data sources, provides adjusted income for each sampled household rather than for groups of households. It is only the information by each individual household which permits estimates of the income distribution without statistical bias (see section 5).

For a number of other countries, such as India, Nepal, the Philippines, Sierra Leone, the Sudan, and Trinidad and Tobago, it was not possible to apply consistently one of the above adjustments because sufficient data were not available. As a result, the original data were only partially adjusted, but according to one of the earlier-mentioned adjustment procedures. In tables 1 and 2 these countries are indicated with an asterisk.

Since Altimir's methodology is applied in nine case studies and since it is not well known, it may be appropriate to describe his adjustment methodology in some detail. The underestimation is normally highest for net income from self-employment and capital income, when comparing the aggregate household survey estimates with the corresponding National Accounts totals. The adjustment which Altimir[27] proposes is the following: for income types where aggregate survey estimates are lower than the corresponding National Accounts totals, one adjusts survey income proportionally according to the underestimation with National Accounts. If the survey total is higher, then one retains the survey data. This can happen (and frequently happens) in the case of wages and salaries and particularly of imputed rent. The assumption of proportional correction is likely to have little effect for wages and salaries and transfer income, because they are normally well captured by the survey. In the case of net income from self-employment, the assumption is reasonable because the underestimation is the result of the long recall period (normally one year) and some voluntary under-reporting out of fear of taxation. For capital income the difference between National Accounts and aggregated survey data is completely attributed to the highest quintile of the household available income distribution - a fixed proportion of household available income. The reason for the different treatment of capital (or investment) income is that the underestimation is likely to be due to deliberate under-reporting of the highest income groups, while this is not the case for lower income classes. The choice of the highest quintile of households is, however, somewhat arbitrary. It would be better to attribute the underestimated income to the richest primary income earners and to determine what proportion of them is likely to under-report for each individual country; but the data are lacking to undertake this type of adjustment.

3. Results

Table 1 shows the main results of this study, i.e. (better) comparable household income distribution data for 23 developed and developing countries. It indicates the deciles of households and the gini index calculated from the decile distribution. For some countries it was not possible to use the exact concept of "available income", but rather "household income before tax", or available income excluding imputed rent. The inclusion of direct taxes and/or the exclusion of imputed rent are not likely to influence the income distribution very much. Particularly in developing countries, personal income taxes are only a small proportion of total income; in addition, imputed rent is usually a fixed proportion of income in all income classes. Table 2 shows the per head distributions for the 14 countries for which these distributions could be estimated. It should be mentioned that these distributions are calculated from tables which cross-classify households according to household available income and household size. Measured income inequality is a little lower than its "true" value because households with slightly different incomes are grouped into the cells of the table. As a result, measured inequality cannot capture inequality within cells. However, as section 5 will show, these deviations are very small.

A comparison of table 1 and table 2 shows that the per head distribution is normally somewhat more equal than the per household distribution (except for Kenya and Mexico). As will be shown in the next section, this is explained by the relatively low value of the so-called "economies-of-scale" factor in these two countries.

4. A simple methodology to estimate
   equivalent scales

In five case studies (Denmark, Federal Republic of Germany, Ireland, Mexico, United Kingdom) we have tried to estimate the distribution of persons by household available income per equivalent unit. Although there are various ways to estimate equivalent scales,[28] we have chosen a simple methodology which can be applied to most available data sets, in both developed and developing countries.

In the literature about equivalent scales, most authors make a clear distinction between equivalent scales and economies of scale in household consumption. Equivalent scales indicate the relative needs of persons of different age and sex. It is commonly assumed that an adult man needs more income to satisfy his needs (for food, housing and clothing, for example) than a child of, say, 10 years old. Another unrelated concept refers to economies of scale in household consumption. Such economies of scale occur, for example, with renting a house or an apartment. The larger the number of persons living in a house, the smaller will be the housing cost per person.

There are econometric procedures which can estimate these two effects separately.[30] To that end, one would need a large amount of information about each household: not only its composition by age and sex, but also household expenditure disaggregated by various items. This information is normally not available for the countries included in this monograph.

We shall therefore try to estimate the so-called "economies-of-scale factor", which can be easily derived from a double-log food expenditure function. However, this factor includes the effects not only of economies-of-scale household consumption but also of equivalent scales. In other words, this factor measures the joint impact of both effects, although it is not possible to separate them. As we shall see in the chapter on the Federal Republic of Germany, the application of the economies-of-scale factor leads to equivalent scales which are very similar to those found in other OECD countries.

The double-log food expenditure function has the following specification:

$$\log F = a + b \log Y + c \log N \qquad (1)$$

where F = food expenditure per household
Y = available household income
N = household size

If one assumes that a household's level of living varies inversely with the proportion of its expenditure that it devotes to food[29] (F/Y), one can mathematically derive that the equivalent economies-of-scale factor e:

$$(e = \partial \log Y / \partial \log N \text{ for } d(F/Y) = 0) \text{ equals } (c/1-b)$$

By reformulating the food expenditure function it is also possible to directly estimate the scale factor t which is related to e:

$$\log (F/N) = a + b \log (Y/N) - t \log N \qquad (2)$$

As t = 1 - b - c, one can derive that

$$e = 1 - \frac{t}{1-b} \qquad (3)$$

since 0 < b < 1 in the case of food expenditure. One can further derive that if:

t > 0   e < 1   there are economies of scale;

t = 0   e = 1   there are no economies of scale;

t 0   e = 1   there are diseconomies of scale.

This means that if t is significantly different from zero, the economies-of-scale factor e is significantly different from zero.

In general there is a problem with estimating functions (1) and (2) because there is collinearity between log Y and log N and probably even more so between log (Y/N) and log N. As a result we shall use the estimates of e derived from equation (1). In practice, however, the estimates based on equation (2) are usually not much different. It should further be noted that we have always used adjusted household available income as income variable in equations (1) and (2).

The economies-of-scale factor will generally vary between zero and one. If its value is one, then the household income per head distribution is the "optimal" distribution; if its value is zero, then this is so for the household income distribution.

The actual values for the economies-of-scale factor found for various countries vary between 0.563 in Mexico and 0.866 for the United Kingdom. This means that the per head distribution in the United Kingdom is likely to be closer to the "optimal" income distribution than in Mexico. It is not possible to deduce from these figures whether it is the per head or the per household distribution which is closest to the distribution of persons by houshold available income per equivalent unit. We shall come back to this issue in section 5.

5. Transition matrices and statistical
    bias as a result of grouped data

    (a) Transition matrices

In section 1 we argued that the person is a more appropriate recipient unit than the household. In the previous section we saw that in some cases measured inequality of the distribution of household income is closer to the distribution of persons by equivalent income than the distribution by per head income. With the help of so-called transition matrices we would like to find out, for those countries for which appropriate data are available, which distribution could be considered as second best.

The transition matrix is defined as the distribution of persons (or households)[31] ranked in deciles according to two income measures. Given the fact that we consider three of such measures (i.e. household available income per household, per head and per equivalent unit), there are three transition matrices for each data set.

Table 3: Sum of diagonal elements ("trace") of various transition matrices in deciles of persons (percentages) – economies-of-scale factors

| | Income concept* | | | | | | Economies-of-scale factor |
| | Original data | | | Adjusted data | | | |
	I/II (1)	I/III (2)	II/III (3)	I/II (4)	I/III (5)	II/III (6)	(7)
Denmark (1976)	12.3	15.3	37.4	14.6	15.6	35.4	0.664
France (1975)	23.6	27.9	69.0	23.6	33.2	66.5	n.a.
Germany (Fed.Rep.) (1974)	n.a.	n.a.	n.a.	17.0	23.8	41.0	0.632
Mexico (1968)	34.3	52.0	54.6	41.4	54.8	62.5	0.563
United Kingdom (1979)	14.0	18.1	60.6	13.6	17.0	69.3	0.866

* Household available income: I - per household; II - per head; III - per equivalent unit.

Note: The "traces" are calculated on the basis of tables cross-classifying household available income and household size (80-100 cells).

We are particularly interested to know whether persons stay in the same decile irrespective of the income measure. A convenient way of measuring this is the sum of the diagonal elements ("trace") which indicates the percentage of persons that remain in the same decile (see table 3). The trace can be considered as a simplified ranking correlation coefficient.

Table 3, which is based on grouped data,[32] shows that the trace is highest for the transition matrices combining household available income per head and per equivalent unit. It is therefore justified to conclude that - at least for the countries shown in table 3 - the per head distribution is the "second-best" distribution. The last column of table 3 shows the economies-of-scale factors. Comparing the last column with the first six columns shows that a high economies-of-scale factor (such as for the United Kingdom) corresponds with a large difference between, respectively, columns (1), (2), (4), (5) and columns (3), (6), while the opposite is also true (see figures for Mexico). In other words, a high economies-of-scale factor means that the "optimal" income distribution is close to that of the per head distribution (i.e. no economies of scale). It may be that in semi-developed and developing countries, such as Mexico,[33] economies of scale in consumption expenditure are more important. For the countries included in this monograph we did not find that the economies-of-scale factor (e) was lower than 0.5. In the extreme case of e = 0 (maximum economies of scale), the "optimal" distribution would be the same as the household distribution. The values found for the various countries seem acceptable. We have shown that the economies-of-scale factor calculated for the Federal Republic of Germany, for example, lead to equivalent scales which are remarkably similar to the OECD scales for industrialised market-economy countries.

(b) Statistical bias as a result
    of grouped data

In section 3 we mentioned in passing that there may be an important difference between inequality measured on the basis of grouped data (in our case tables cross-classifying households and persons by household income and household size) and inequality measured on the basis of individual household observations. We were fortunate to have available the individual household observations of the 1968 Mexican survey, so that we can analyse the differences between both data sets. There are two types of bias that we would like to investigate here. The first relates to the distribution of income per head and per equivalent unit and the second to the adjustment of income.

The first type of bias arises when one derives the distribution of income per head and per equivalent unit on the basis of grouped data. If one compares these distributions with those based on individual household data, one finds a remarkably small difference.

Table 4: Mexico (1968). Gini-indices and decile distributions of
incomes adjusted for national accounts. Two ranking
criteria: unadjusted income and adjusted income

Ranking criterion	Unadjusted income			Adjusted income		
Income concept*	I	II	III	I	II	III
Recipient unit	Household (1)	Person (2)	Person (3)	Household (4)	Person (5)	Person (6)
Deciles						
I	0.8	0.8	0.9	0.7	0.7	0.7
II	2.2	2.0	2.3	2.0	1.9	2.0
III	2.9	2.9	3.0	2.8	2.6	2.8
IV	3.8	3.6	3.9	3.6	3.5	3.6
V	4.7	4.5	4.7	4.5	4.4	4.5
VI	5.9	5.9	6.0	5.7	5.7	5.9
VII	7.4	7.6	7.5	7.5	7.4	7.8
VIII	10.6	9.7	10.4	10.6	9.9	10.3
IX	16.1	16.1	15.7	15.9	15.5	15.7
X	45.5	47.0	45.5	46.7	48.5	46.7
Gini index	0.55	0.56	0.54	0.56	0.58	0.56

* I: household available income;
 II: household available income per capita;
III: household available income per equivalent unit.

The gini index calculated with the individual household data is 0.540 for the per head distribution (compared with 0.535 based on grouped data) and is 0.521 for the per equivalent distribution (compared with 0.518 based on grouped data).

The second type of bias arises when we adjust incomes for inconsistencies with National Accounts without being able to rerank income recipients according to adjusted income. This creates a bias which was recently investigated, in a somewhat different context, by Pyatt, Chen and Fei.[34] If we define adjusted income $(y_i{}^*)$ as the sum of unadjusted income (y_i) and a correction factor (u_i), i.e. $y_i{}^* = y_i + u_i$, we are interested to know whether the ranking of adjusted income $r(y_i{}^*)$ equals that of unadjusted income $r(y_i)$

or whether $r(u_i) = r(y_i)$.

In most cases the adjustment is proportional to observed income so that:

$$y_{ik}{}^* = (1 + c_k)y_{ik}, \text{ where k refers to type of income.}$$

The question now is: under what conditions is it true that $r(u_i) = r(y_i)$? Three exceptional cases exist. Firstly, if $u_i = 0$ - in other words - if no adjustment takes place. Secondly, if $u_i = Cy_i$, i.e. if the adjustment is the same for each factor income and, thirdly, if $r(y_{ik}) = r(y_i)$, i.e. if the ranking of each factor income is the same as that for total income.

In the case of Mexico, the last condition is broadly fulfilled for wages and salaries and income from self-employment (looking at deciles). Together these two income sources represent about three-quarters of household income. Since we allocate underestimated income from capital to the highest quintile of households, this is not likely to disturb the ranking either. Finally, the ranking of transfer income is almost opposite to that of total household income and is, therefore, likely to disturb the ranking. However, since transfer incomes represent only 5 per cent of household income, it is not likely to have a great impact (table 4).

We also checked for a number of other countries (Denmark, France, Ireland, Spain, Sweden, United Kingdom) to determine whether the adjustments are likely to influence the ranking of recipient units. Our conclusion is that this is probably not the case because wages and salaries usually constitute between 80 and 90 per cent of household available income and the adjustment on this type of income is small. The adjustment on income from self-employment and capital is normally larger, but its value generally increases with available household income. As a result, the ranking is not disturbed (except in Sweden, where capital income is also concentrated in low-income pensioners). The adjustment of transfer incomes, income taxes and social security contributions could disturb the ranking, but their share in average household available income is normally not higher than 30 per cent.

We do not expect any ranking problems either for those countries where consumption expenditure and savings were adjusted separately (see the estimates for Egypt, the Islamic Republic of Iran and Tanzania), because savings increase progressively with household income (and with household expenditure). Ranking problems are also not likely to occur in the cases of Kenya and Zambia, where the adjusted distribution was estimated on the basis of a log-normal distribution. There may be problems with the estimates for countries where the adjustment was only partial (India and Trinidad and Tobago) or where the proportion of under-reported income is a large proportion of total income, i.e. more than 30 per cent (Ireland, Mexico, Philippines, Spain, Sudan, Tanzania, Trinidad and Tobago).

6. Future research

The 23 new income distribution estimates may be somewhat more consistent than those generated before. However, they represent far-from-perfect estimates and there are various ways in which they could be improved.

It is a truism to say that income distribution estimates are more reliable when they are based on good surveys, and that they are more comparable when those surveys use similar income and income unit concepts. Within the World Bank it is the project on Living Standards Measurement Study (LSMS) which is deeply involved in the question of concepts. This focuses mainly on formulating the core of questions and underlying concepts which will permit statements about the changes over time in the main elements of living standards subject to policy interventions. The greatest source of comparable information on income distribution will come from the United Nations National Household Survey Capability Programme, in which also the ILO is involved actively.

Adjustments for inconsistencies with reliable National Accounts and population data will be needed less, as the underlying household data are of better quality. We have seen that wages and salaries as well as government transfers are usually well captured by the survey, but not the incomes from self-employment and investment. It is particularly difficult to estimate the capital income of the highest income classes. Various countries have already started to set up so-called Social Accounting Matrices (SAMs) which combine information traditionally included in National Accounts with disaggregated information on income classes and/or socio-economic groups. To construct a SAM, all sorts of data can be used, such as tax and social security data, household surveys, National Accounts, censuses, etc.

The most advanced way of adjusting is a so-called merge-file (see section 2) which includes adjusted income and other data for each individual household observation. It is only this type of information which permits income distribution estimates without statistical bias. However, as was shown in section 5, this bias is usually small, if sufficiently detailed cross-classifications are available.

Notes

[1] See, for example, D. McGranahan: International comparability of statistics on income distribution (Geneva, United Nations Research Institute for Social Development, 1979).

[2] I. Adelman and C.F. Morris: Economic growth and social equity in developing countries (Stanford, California, Stanford University Press, 1973).

[3] F. Paukert: "Income distribution at different levels of development: A survey of evidence", in International Labour Review (Geneva, ILO), Aug.-Sep. 1973, pp. 97-125.

[4] S. Jain: Size distribution of income: A compilation of data (Washington, DC, World Bank, 1975).

[5] M. Sawyer: Income distribution in OECD countries, Occasional Studies, OECD Economic Outlook (Paris, July 1976).

[6] P. Visaria: Poverty and living standards in Asia: An overview of the main results and lessons of selected household surveys, Living Standards Measurement Study Working Paper No. 2 (Washington, DC, World Bank, 1980; mimeographed).

[7] O. Altimir and J.V. Sourrouille: Measuring levels of living in Latin America: An overview of main problems, Living Standards Measurement Study Working Paper No. 3 (Washington, DC, World Bank, 1980; mimeographed).

[8] J. Lecaillon, F. Paukert, C. Morrisson and D. Germidis: Income distribution and economic development: An analytical survey (Geneva, ILO, 1984).

[9] United Nations Statistical Office: A survey of national sources of income distribution statistics (New York, 1981).

[10] United Nations: Provisional guide-lines in statistics of the distribution of income, consumption and accumulation of households, Studies in Methods, Series M, No. 61 (New York, 1977). See also ILO: International recommendations on labour statistics (Geneva, 1975).

[11] H. Lydall: Effects of alternative measurement techniques on the estimation of the inequality of income (Geneva, ILO, 1981; mimeographed World Employment Programme research working paper; restricted), p. 11.

[12] United Nations: Draft principles and recommendations for population and housing censuses (New York, 1978; document E/CN.3/515/Add.2), paras. 73-74.

[13] S. Danziger and M.K. Taussig: "The income unit and the anatomy of income distribution", in Review of Income and Wealth (New Haven, Connecticut), Dec. 1979, pp. 365-375.

[14] A.K. Sen: Three notes on the concept of poverty (Geneva, ILO, 1978; mimeographed World Employment Programme research working paper; restricted), p. 17.

[15] For an application of this principle, see W. van Ginneken: "Some methods of poverty analysis: An application to Iranian data 1975-1976", in World Development (Oxford, Pergamon Press), Sep. 1980, pp. 639-646.

[16] Sen, op. cit.

[17] It is pointed out by Deaton and Muellbauer that one really needs a theory of allocation within the household. The assumption of the equivalent unit estimation assumes that the available household income is spent in proportion to the equivalent value that each household member represents. This may not be realistic given the fact that in many developing countries women and children receive less than their equivalent unit share. See A. Deaton and J. Muellbauer: Economics and consumer behaviour (Cambridge, Cambridge University Press, 1980), p. 227.

[18] O. Altimir: Income distribution estimates from household surveys and population censuses in Latin America: An assessment of reliability (Washington, DC, World Bank, Development Research Center, 1977; mimeographed).

[19] ibid., p. 95.

[20] P.D. Ojha and V.V. Bhatt: "Pattern of income distribution in India: 1953-55 to 1963-65", in Sankhya (Calcutta), Vol. 36, Series C, 1974, pp. 163-166.

[21] K.R. Ranadive: Distribution of income trends since planning, paper presented at the ISI seminar on income distribution (Calcutta, 1973).

[22] I. de Navarrete: "La distribución del ingreso en México: tendencias y perspectivas" in El perfil de México en 1980 (Mexico, DF, 3rd ed., 1971), Vol. 1, pp. 15-62.

[23] See also W. van Ginneken: Socio-economic groups and income distribution in Mexico (London, Croom Helm, 1980).

[24] See for example, G. Pyatt and E. Thorbecke: Planning techniques for a better future (Geneva, ILO, 1976).

[25] A good example is the income distribution estimates by the Deutsches Institute für Wirtschaftsforschung; see G. Göseke and K.D. Bedau: Verteilung und Schichtung der Einkommen der privaten Haushalte in der Bundesrepublik Deutschland 1950 bis 1975 (Distribution and classification of private household incomes in the Federal Republic of Germany, 1950 to 1975) (Berlin, DIW, 1974).

[26] K. Kortmann: "Die Generierung einer geschlossen Mikrodatenbasis für die Bundesrepublik Deutschland" (The generation of a closed microdata file for the Federal Republic of Germany), in H.-J. Krupp and W. Glatzer (eds.): Umverteilung in Sozialstaat (Redistribution in the welfare state) (Frankfurt, 1978), pp. 193-236. For a description of an American merge-file, see J.A. Pechman and B.A. Okner: Who bears the tax burden? (Washington, DC, the Brookings Institution, 1974), Appendix A. This file is regularly updated and the latest available data refer to 1975.

[27] O. Altimir: Income distribution estimates ..., op. cit.

[28] See for example, T. Goedhart, V. Halberstadt, A. Kapteyn and B. van Praag: "The poverty line: Concept and measurement", in Journal of Human Resources (Madison, Wisconsin, University of Wisconsin Press), Fall 1977, pp. 503-520, and J.L. Nicholson: "Appraisal of different methods of estimating equivalent scales and their results", in Review of Income and Wealth (New Haven, Connecticut), Mar. 1976, pp. 1-11.

[29] A recent, more sophisticated, way to estimate equivalent scales on the basis of food shares is presented by A. Deaton and J. Muellbauer, op. cit., pp. 205-212. They propose to consider the food share as a function of the logarithm of total expenditure. This has the advantage that the sum of expenditures on all items adds up to total expenditure and that equivalent scales are a function of total expenditures. The methodology was applied to Sri Lanka data. See A. Deaton: Three essays on a Sri Lanka household survey, Living Standards Measurement Study Working Paper No. 11 (Washington, DC, World Bank; mimeographed).

[30] See for example, Y.S. Cramer: Empirical econometrics (Amsterdam, North-Holland Publishing Co., 1969).

[31] We shall not show the transition matrices for households which are normally quite similar to those for persons.

[32] W. van Ginneken: Comparable income distribution data for Mexico (1968), United Kingdom (1979) and the Federal Republic of Germany, (1974) (Geneva, ILO, 1981; mimeographed World Employment Programme research working paper; restricted), p. 48. See also W. van Ginneken: "Generating internationally comparable income distribution data: Evidence from the Federal Republic of Germany (1974), Mexico (1968) and the United Kingdom (1969), in Review of Income and Wealth, Dec. 1968, pp. 365-379.

[33] For Mexico we also calculated transition matrices on the basis of individual household data. The "traces" calculated on this basis are not much different from those of table 1 (nor more than two percentage points).

[34] G. Pyatt, C. Chen, J. Fei: "The distribution of income by factor components", in Quarterly Journal of Economics (New York, John Wiley), Nov. 1980, pp. 451-473.

II. COUNTRY ESTIMATES

The results shown in the first part of this monograph are based on individual country case studies. The studies undertaken by staff members or collaborators of the World Bank were brought out as Division working papers of the Economic and Social Data Division of the Economic Analysis and Projections Department (EPD). The studies undertaken by staff members or collaborators of the ILO were published either as World Employment Programme research working papers or as individual mimeographed papers. The 23-country chapters that follow are a summary of those papers.

At the beginning of each chapter we have inserted a short summary which indicates the data source, the income concept used, the adjustment procedure and the types of income distribution estimates that were generated.

At the end of the 23-country chapters we attach a short appendix which shows, for a number of countries, income distribution estimates that are comparable to those described in this monograph.

1. BANGLADESH (1973-74)

(S. Kansal, World Bank, Washington, DC)

Summary

The income distribution estimate for Bangladesh is based on the 1973-74 Household Expenditure Survey (HES). It was not necessary to adjust income data for inconsistencies with National Accounts because aggregated household income before tax derived from the survey was about equal to the corresponding National Accounts' total. It was, however, necessary to adjust the household composition by size because large households tended to be over-represented in the sample. The study estimated distributions of gross (i.e. before tax) available income per household and per head, both in rural and urban areas.

The 1973-74 Household Expenditure Survey (HES), conducted by the Bangladesh Bureau of Statistics, was used to derive the estimates of household income distribution. Prior to the establishment of Bangladesh in 1971, the Central Statistical Office of Pakistan had periodically conducted household income and expenditure surveys. The last survey report pertains to the year 1966-67. This brief provides income distribution estimates for 1973-74 and compares these with similar estimates for 1966-67.

1. Brief description of the 1973-74 survey

The 1973-74 survey covered private households in all rural and urban areas of Bangladesh, excluding institutional households such as boarding houses, hostels, hospitals, etc. The sample included 11,773 households (9,536 rural and 2,237 urban), or about 0.09 per cent of total private households. The survey was conducted between July 1973 and June 1974. The reference period for wages and salaries, professional fees, etc. was the month prior to the date of the interview; for interest receipts, dividends, agricultural and business income and gifts, etc. the previous year was defined as the reference period. The tabulated data gave average monthly household incomes during the survey period.

A household was defined as consisting of one or more persons normally living and eating together in the same dwelling unit. Household incomes included the before-tax incomes of all members of the household (excluding boarders and domestic workers). Cash income and receipts in kind were included. Consumption of home-produced goods, imputed rents from owner-occupied dwellings, gifts, assistance in kind, etc., were valued at market prices and were included in household income.

2. Evaluation of the 1973-74 survey

The income concept used in the survey was similar to the total household income concept defined in the United Nations guide-lines, with the exception that the survey excluded the income of boarders and domestic workers.

The survey report does not give any information on the non-enumeration rate.[1] It only states the number of sample households for which data were processed. There seems, however, to have been considerable non-enumeration, as the survey estimate of the total number of households was considerably lower than the number of households enumerated in the census of population.

A comparison of the distribution of sample households by size with similar census data suggests that while small-sized households were under-represented, large-sized households were over-represented in the sample. Since average household income seemed to increase with an increase in household size, it is likely that the survey estimate of overall average household income was overestimated. This assumption was confirmed by the fact that the survey estimate of total household income was 5 per cent higher (72,700 million Taka) than a similar estimate based on national accounts data (69,000 million Taka).

The survey estimate of the total number of urban households was much lower than the census figure of total urban households. Thus, the survey estimate of income distribution for all of Bangladesh, which was derived by combining the urban and rural income distributions, was biased towards the rural income distribution.

3. Derivation of income distribution

As noted, the distribution of sample households was biased towards large-sized households. The survey data were adjusted for this bias in three steps. First, the sample proportions of one- and two-person households were increased to those of the census, thereby reducing the proportion of "ten or more person" households. Second, the adjusted number of sample households in each household size group were distributed among various income classes in the same proportions as were observed in the original sample. Finally, the adjusted distribution of household income was derived by aggregating the revised sample households in each household size group for each income class; this was done separately for rural and urban areas.

National household income distribution was derived by aggregating the rural and urban income distributions, using the census estimate of the total number of households in the two areas as weights. Table 1.1 gives the household income distribution by deciles of households and the gini index for rural, urban and all of Bangladesh.

Table 1.1: Distribution of adjusted gross household available income by households (in percentages), Bangladesh, 1973-74

Deciles (households)	Rural	Urban	Combined
I	2.7	2.7	2.7
II	4.1	4.0	4.1
III	5.2	5.0	5.1
IV	6.3	6.0	6.3
V	7.8	6.9	7.6
VI	8.4	8.3	8.5
VII	10.1	10.5	10.2
VIII	13.6	11.1	13.3
IX	14.7	16.2	14.8
X	27.2	29.3	27.4
Gini index	0.35	0.38	0.35

Table 1.2: Distribution of adjusted gross household available income per capita by persons (in percentages), Bangladesh, 1973-74

Deciles (persons)	Rural	Urban	Combined
I	3.6	3.4	3.6
II	5.3	5.2	5.2
III	6.4	5.9	6.4
IV	7.3	7.0	7.2
V	8.6	8.1	8.5
VI	9.4	8.6	9.4
VII	10.4	9.8	10.2
VIII	11.9	11.9	11.7
IX	14.4	14.8	14.4
X	22.7	25.3	23.4
Gini index	0.28	0.31	0.28

Table 1.3: Distribution of gross household available income by households (in percentages), Bangladesh, 1966-67 and 1973-74

Household groups	Per cent of household income	
	1966-67[1]	1973-74[2]
Lowest 20%	8.7	6.9
2nd quintile	10.9	11.3
3rd quintile	14.6	16.1
4th quintile	21.7	23.5
Highest 20%	44.1	42.2
Highest 10%	29.5	27.4
Gini index	0.34	0.36

[1] Taken from A.K.M. Ghulam Rabbani and Shadat Hussain: Rural and urban consumption patterns in contemporary Bangladesh (Bangladesh Bureau of Statistics, Statistics Division, Ministry of Planning, Dacca, May 1978), pp. 2-6.

[2] The income data have been slightly adjusted (see text).

The survey report contains a two-way table showing the distribution of sample households by household size and income class. Average per head household income in each cell was computed by dividing the average household income with the corresponding size of the household. The per head household income distribution was derived by reclassifying the household members according to per head household income. Table 1.2 gives per head income distribution by deciles of population and the gini index for rural, urban and all of Bangladesh.

The gini index was much lower on a per head basis (0.28) than on a household basis (0.36).

4.   Comparison over time

A review of the 1966-67 survey report suggests that the data from that survey are broadly comparable with the 1973-74 survey estimates, as both used similar concepts, definitions, coverage and income classes.   Table 1.3 provides the income distribution by quintiles of households and the gini index for 1966-67, which have not been adjusted and those for 1973-74, which were slightly adjusted (for the original data, see the appendix).   It seems that income inequality hardly changed between 1966 and 1974.

5.   Concluding remarks

Income inequality in Bangladesh is relatively low as compared with that of other developing countries.   Further, the level of inequality does not seem to have changed significantly between 1966-67 and 1973-74.

Note

[1] Non-emuneration includes non-response.   Other reasons for non-enumeration could have been either a vacant house or the inability of the enumerator to contact the sample household.

Appendix 1.1: Distribution of sample households by monthly gross household income and household size; rural Bangladesh 1973-74

Monthly house-hold income class (Taka)	Average household income (Taka)	Number of house-holds		One	Two	Three	Four	Five	Six	Seven	Eight	Nine	Ten or more
Less than 50	30	12	a	30	15	10	7	--	--	--	--	--	--
			b	6	3	1	2	--	--	--	--	--	--
50- 99	80	164	a	80	40	27	20	16	13	11	10	--	7
			b	42	41	30	21	10	11	5	2	--	2
100- 149	126	537	a	126	63	42	32	25	21	18	16	14	16
			b	41	136	132	101	74	26	15	9	2	1
150- 199	174	868	a	174	87	58	44	35	29	25	22	19	12
			b	22	144	211	186	142	85	53	15	7	3
200- 249	224	1 016	a	224	112	75	56	45	37	32	28	25	23
			b	15	137	219	239	183	124	50	33	5	11
250- 299	273	971	a	273	137	91	68	55	46	39	34	30	25
			b	4	76	174	215	208	150	77	40	15	12
300- 399	346	1 673	a	346	173	115	87	69	58	49	43	38	31
			b	7	88	191	304	356	333	208	104	43	39
400- 499	445	1 228	a	445	223	148	111	89	74	64	56	49	41
			b	6	19	100	180	248	247	196	130	42	60

	a/b	500– 749	750– 999	1 000–1 499	1 500–1 999	2 000 and above	All cases	Average household income
	a	53	74	93	126	210	83	710
	b	205	202	236	52	50	873	
	a	67	96	133	188	359	79	577
	b	154	92	47	8	5	420	
	a	75	108	149	212	––	72	525
	b	264	104	53	6	––	760	
	a	86	123	171	242	462	75	446
	b	344	106	55	3	4	1 116	
	a	101	144	199	282	539	74	393
	b	327	67	38	3	4	1 415	
	a	121	172	239	339	647	79	333
	b	257	51	16	6	5	1 556	
	a	151	215	298	424	808	83	285
	b	158	26	11	1	1	1 445	
	a	201	287	398	565	1 078	95	223
	b	66	9	5	3	1	1 142	
	a	302	436	597	––	––	112	184
	b	12	2	2	––	––	660	
	a	604	––	1 194	1 695	––	184	
	b	4	––	1	1	––	149	
All cases	a	604	862	1 194	1 695	3 233	464	464
	b	1 791	659	464	83	70	9 536	––
Average household income								1 004

Note: 'a' denotes average monthly per head income in Taka; 'b' denotes number of sample households.

Source: A Report on the Household Expenditure Survey of Bangladesh, 1973-74, (Dhaka, Bangladesh Bureau of Statistics, Statistics Division, Ministry of Planning, Aug. 1978), Vol. I.

Appendix 1.2: Distribution of sample households by monthly gross household income and household size; urban Bangladesh, 1973-74

Monthly household income class (Taka)	Average household income (Taka)	Number of households		Size of household									
				One	Two	Three	Four	Five	Six	Seven	Eight	Nine	Ten or more
Less than 50	--	--	a	--	--	--	--	--	--	--	--	--	--
			b	--	--	--	--	--	--	--	--	--	--
50- 99	78	15	a	78	39	26	19	16	13	--	--	--	8
			b	5	2	2	1	1	3	--	--	--	1
100- 149	128	43	a	128	64	43	32	26	21	18	--	14	--
			b	6	13	15	3	2	2	1	--	1	--
150- 199	173	107	a	173	86	58	43	35	29	25	22	19	14
			b	8	13	24	23	19	8	5	4	1	2
200- 249	222	175	a	222	111	74	56	44	37	32	28	25	18
			b	12	26	29	36	29	18	9	6	4	6
250- 299	270	181	a	270	135	90	68	54	45	39	34	30	24
			b	17	13	26	28	40	24	14	9	6	4
300- 399	344	372	a	344	172	115	86	69	57	49	43	38	33
			b	5	18	45	71	76	60	47	34	7	9
400- 499	445	291	a	445	222	148	111	89	74	64	56	49	42
			b	3	12	22	34	46	58	47	35	11	23

Income class													
500- 749	483	605	a	605	302	202	151	121	101	86	76	67	53
			b	1	6	23	44	65	84	86	63	47	64
750- 999	228	852	a	--	--	284	213	170	142	122	107	95	77
			b	--	--	5	10	24	32	35	29	24	69
1 000-1 499	224	1 187	a	--	1 187	396	297	237	198	170	148	132	96
			b	--	1	1	9	14	19	23	25	26	106
1 500-1 999	62	1 682	a	--	--	561	421	336	280	240	210	187	124
			b	--	--	1	3	2	3	7	7	9	30
2 000 and above	56	3 243	a	--	--	1 621	--	649	540	463	405	360	219
			b	--	--	1	--	3	3	3	2	5	39
All classes	2 237	630	a	252	153	114	105	98	92	90	83	96	97
			b	58	104	193	262	321	314	277	214	140	353
Average household 1 180 income	630		--	--	252	305	342	421	489	555	630	666	866

Note: 'a' denotes average monthly per head income in Taka; 'b' denotes number of sample households.

Source: As in Appendix 1.1

2. <u>DENMARK</u> (1976)

(W. van Ginneken, ILO, Geneva)

<u>Summary</u>

The Danish income distribution estimates are based on the 1976 Household Sample Survey. The income concept used in this survey is household disposable income, i.e. excluding imputed rent of owner-occupied houses. The original income data were adjusted for inconsistency with National Accounts, by type of income. The study estimated nation-wide distributions of disposable income per household, per head and per equivalent unit.

1. The 1976 household survey

The 1976 sample survey includes 3,000 households. The sample was stratified so as to take account of the distribution of income and consumption. The self-employed were therefore surveyed at twice the frequency of other population groups.

It was not possible to base the sample on the population data from the 1971 census because they were out of date in 1976. It was therefore decided to base the sample on the central register of persons. The sample was based on all household heads more than 18 years old born on the 15th day of a month with an even number.

The 1976 survey defines the household as comprising all those (including cohabitants but excluding domestic servants and lodgers) who share common consumption expenditures. This definition corresponds broadly with the definition used in other countries, but is narrower than the household concept used in the central register of persons. As a result, some of the "households" originally selected were eliminated by some questions in the preliminary interview designed to prevent the size of the household influencing its chances of being selected for the survey.

There is a substantial non-response rate in the survey. To retain the original size and composition of the sample survey, the missing households were replaced by households which are equivalent to those originally selected in terms of socio-economic group, household type and geographical location. Every household figuring in the tabulations was given a weighting, partly to cancel out any discrepancy in selection frequency and partly to correct any imbalance resulting from non-responders for whom no replacements had been found.

The income concept used in the survey is household disposable income, which is not exactly the same as the concept of "household available income" used for other countries. Although the survey concept includes income in kind earned by self-employed workers (mainly shopkeepers and farmers), it does not include imputed rent of owner-occupied houses.

2. Consistency with National Accounts and population data

It is not possible to find directly the National Accounts totals which correspond with the aggregated household data. The following National Accounts data are known to us (supplied by the Danish Statistical Office):

- wages and salaries (including actual and imputed social security contributions) - 140,541 million Danish kroner;

- transfer income to private households from general government - 33,933 million Danish kroner;

- direct taxes - 61,857 million Danish kroner.

The OECD[1] estimates current receipts of households at 204,434 million, so that the sum of entrepreneurial income and property income must be (204,434 - 140,541 - 33,933), which is equal to 29,960 million Danish kroner. Total household disposable income must be equal to current receipts (204,434) minus direct taxes (61,857) minus employers' and employees' contribution (1,640) which together we estimate at 2,750. Total household disposable income therefore equals 139,827 million Danish kroner.

The weighted number of households in the sample amounts to 2,762.6 (see appendix) which include 6,894.5 persons. Since the total population was 5,072,516 on 1 July 1976, one can estimate the total number of households at 2,032,538. The number is used for calculating household survey totals in table 2.1.

It shows that the underestimation of the various income sources is very low. It is unexpected to find that aggregated survey data on net self-employment income and capital income are higher than the corresponding National Accounts data. It should, however, be remembered that the estimation procedure was indirect and should be considered as only tentative.

It was not possible to check whether the distribution of households by household size corresponds with national information sources because the last census only took place in 1971.

Table 2.1: Disposable income from the 1976 survey compared with data derived from the 1976 National Accounts (million Kroner)

Sources of income	1976 survey (1)	National Accounts (2)	100* (1):(2) = (3)
Wages and salaries (including SSS contributions)	139 276	140 541	99.1
Net income from self-employment + capital income	31 517	29 960	105.2
Transfer income	30 722	33 933	90.5
Direct taxes	56 881	61 857	92.0
Disposable household income	144 634	142 577	101.4

Table 2.2: Estimates of double-log food expenditure functions (Denmark, 1976)

						No. of observations (weighted)
Log F	= a	+ b log Y	+ c log N	R^2		
	6.04	0.260	0.491	0.98	0.664	88
		(0.004)	(0.004)			
Log (F/N)	= a	+ b log (Y/N)	- t log N	R^2		
	6.04	0.260	0.249	0.93	0.664	88
		(0.004)	(0.003)			

Note: F = household expenditure on food;
Y = household disposable income (adjusted);
N = household size.

Table 2.3: Distribution of household disposable income (in
percentages). Gini indices and decile distributions (in
percentages). Original data and data adjusted with
National Accounts; per household per capita, and per
equivalent unit. Denmark 1976

Type of data	Original			Adjusted		
Income concept	I	II	III	I	II	III
Recipient unit	Household (1)	Person (2)	Person (3)	Household (4)	Person (5)	Person (6)
Deciles						
I	2.7	3.9	4.4	2.9	4.0	4.4
II	4.3	5.7	5.7	4.5	5.5	6.0
III	5.4	6.3	6.5	5.6	6.4	6.7
IV	6.9	7.3	7.4	7.0	7.3	7.4
V	8.5	7.9	8.4	8.5	8.2	8.5
VI	9.8	8.9	9.4	9.8	9.0	9.4
VII	11.4	10.5	10.6	11.3	10.4	10.6
VIII	13.0	12.1	12.0	12.9	12.2	12.0
IX	15.3	14.8	14.2	15.1	14.7	14.2
X	22.8	22.7	21.3	22.4	22.3	20.8
Gini index	0.31	0.27	0.25	0.30	0.27	0.24

Note: The decile distributions are calculated on the basis of tables
cross-classifying household disposable income(15 classes) and
household size (6 groups).

I: household disposable income;
II: household disposable income per capita;
III: household disposable income per equivalent unit.

Table 2.4: Composition of household disposable income by source, by household income classes (Denmark, 1976) (in percentages)

Deciles (household)	Wages	Net income from self-employment	Capital income	Transfers	Direct taxes	Household disposable income
I	12.7	2.7	7.7	86.3	- 9.4	100.0
II	24.6	21.0	10.1	76.9	-32.6	100.0
III	65.7	12.0	9.5	49.4	-36.6	100.0
IV	71.4	26.5	7.4	33.3	-38.7	100.0
V	91.2	15.9	4.5	25.8	-37.4	100.0
VI	108.7	9.3	5.8	20.8	-44.6	100.0
VII	112.1	10.2	3.3	15.1	-40.8	100.0
VIII	121.5	11.1	3.2	9.4	-45.1	100.0
IX	117.1	13.2	4.3	7.5	-42.0	100.0
X	96.1	28.4	6.1	8.8	-39.3	100.0
Average	96.3	16.4	5.4	21.2	-39.3	100.0

3. Results

We were not able to adjust the data on net income from self-employment and on capital income separately, because the corresponding National Accounts totals were not available. As a result, both sources of income were taken together and adjusted proportionally.

Having adjusted the income data, we estimated the economies-of-scale factor on the basis of double-log food expenditure functions (see table 2.2).

Both estimates lead to the same value for the economies of scale factor (0.664) which was subsequently used to calculate household disposable income per equivalent unit. Table 2.3 shows the main results.

It is unusual to find that the adjusted income distribution is somewhat less unequal than the original income distribution. This is due to the fact that aggregated income from self-employment and capital income as measured by the survey is higher than the corresponding National Accounts total (see table 2.1). Another explanation is that these income sources are concentrated in the higher income classes (see table 2.4).

Note

[1] OECD: National Accounts of OECD countries, 1976 (Paris, 1978), Vol. II, detailed tables, p. 117.

Appendix 2.1: Distribution of sample households (weighted) by disposable household income and household size (Denmark, 1976)

Household disposable income ('000 D.kroner)	Household size						
	1	2	3	4	5	6+	Total
-30	377.7	105.6	18.5	9.2	6.7	2.1	519.8
30-40	100.9	109.4	15.7	7.8	4.2	2.4	240.5
40-50	96.3	115.2	27.1	11.6	8.8	3.9	262.8
50-60	61.5	109.8	39.2	26.3	11.0	1.5	249.2
60-70	23.4	97.9	55.5	59.5	18.7	9.1	264.0
70-80	20.2	108.5	48.6	56.4	23.6	5.3	262.7
80-90	6.4	89.6	52.3	61.9	18.1	11.7	240.0
90-100	5.6	66.4	42.0	52.1	14.2	9.9	190.2
100-110	1.8	54.4	49.5	37.0	18.2	1.4	162.3
110-120	5.2	25.3	26.7	22.2	16.5	2.7	98.5
120-130	3.9	17.2	29.0	23.9	5.7	4.2	83.9
130-140	0.9	13.2	16.0	18.6	7.1	1.6	57.4
140-150	-	5.4	10.0	15.7	4.7	1.1	36.9
150-160	-	6.2	6.5	8.4	5.2	1.0	27.2
160-	3.2	20.8	14.2	18.0	8.0	2.8	67.0
Total	707.1	944.9	450.6	428.5	170.8	60.7	2 762.6

3. EGYPT (1974-75)

(Karima Korayem, El-Ashar University, Cairo)

Summary

The Egyptian income distribution estimates are based on the 1974-75 Household Budget Survey. Aggregated household consumption expenditure derived from this survey is almost equal to the corresponding National Accounts total, while aggregated savings are much lower. Adjusted savings are distributed over households with the help of separate savings equations for urban and rural areas. The study estimated the distributions of available income per household and per head, in both urban and rural areas.

1. Introduction

The only official source available in Egypt is the 1974-75 Employment Sample Survey.[1] However, evaluation of these data shows that they are significantly underestimated as compared with the National Accounts. An alternative source is the 1974-75 Household Budget Sample Survey[2] which only includes information on consumption expenditure per household and per head in urban and rural areas and by expenditure brackets. The sample for this survey consists of 12,000 households, 8,000 in urban and 4,000 in rural areas. The urban sample was allocated to the governorates according to the relative size of the urban population in these governorates. The rural sample is based on a randomly chosen 2 per cent of the villages in each governorate, with a minimum of three villages in any governorate. The rural sample was then distributed to the chosen villages according to their relative population size. The household concept used in this survey corresponds with the United Nations definition, while consumption expenditure includes expenditure in kind, such as imputed rent of owner-occupied housing and the consumption of own produce. Since aggregate consumption expenditure as measured by the latter survey deviates from the National Accounts estimate by only about 5 per cent, it was decided to use the 1974-75 Household Budget Survey as a basis for estimating the distribution of income.

2. The estimation of the savings and consumption expenditure functions

Since the consumption expenditure is well captured in the household budget survey, it is necessary to estimate the savings to get the available income distribution. To do that, the savings and consumption functions are estimated in urban and rural areas, for both households and individuals. Section 3 will then explain how one can calculate savings on the basis of consumption expenditure data.

One can distinguish two lines of thought in the literature about the consumption and saving behaviour of individuals or households: the Keynesian line of thought, which states that consumption and savings depend on current income; and the other line of thought (represented mainly by Friedman's "permanent income hypothesis", Modigliani's "life-cycle hypothesis" and Duesenberry's "relative income hypothesis"), which states that consumption and saving do not depend on current income only, but on other factors as well (e.g. expected average income, transitory income, peak income, age).[3] Since saving and consumption behaviour are strongly inter-related, the forms of the saving function formulated according to these two lines of thought may be applied to the consumption function.[4] The application of the "permanent income hypothesis" means that savings are not only a function of current income (Y_t) but also of lagged income (Y_{t-1}) or lagged savings (S_{t-1}). To estimate the saving and consumption functions, the author experimented with various functional forms. The data used in the regression cover the period between 1966/67 and 1976 and were taken from the National Accounts (savings, consumption expenditure and personal disposable income) and from population estimates (number of households and household size). The experiments show that the best functional form fitting household and per head consumption expenditure in urban and rural areas is the linear function $C_t = a+b\ Y_t$, while the most appropriate savings function appears to be $S_t = C+d\ Y_t + e\ S_{t-1}$. The estimated saving and consumption functions are as follows:

(1) $\quad S_t^{uh} = -82.871 + \underset{(0.041)}{0.202}\ Y_t^{uh} + \underset{(0.185)}{0.208}\ S_{t-1}^{uh} \qquad \bar{R}^2 = 0.887 \\ \qquad\qquad\qquad\qquad\qquad\qquad\qquad\qquad\qquad\qquad\qquad DW = 2.01$

(2) $\quad C_t^{uh} = 82.591 + \underset{(0.047)}{0.785}\ Y_t^{uh} \qquad\qquad\qquad\qquad \bar{R}^2 = 0.972 \\ \qquad\qquad\qquad\qquad\qquad\qquad\qquad\qquad\qquad\qquad\qquad DW = 0.77$

(3) $\quad S_t^{rh} = -47.192 + \underset{(0.039)}{0.177}\ Y_t^{rh} + \underset{(0.198)}{0.253}\ S_{t-1}^{rh} \qquad \bar{R}^2 = 0.878 \\ \qquad\qquad\qquad\qquad\qquad\qquad\qquad\qquad\qquad\qquad\qquad DW = 2.08$

(4) $\quad C_t^{rh} = 46.429 + \underset{(0.043)}{0.811}\ Y_t^{rh} \qquad\qquad\qquad\qquad \bar{R}^2 = 0.978 \\ \qquad\qquad\qquad\qquad\qquad\qquad\qquad\qquad\qquad\qquad\qquad DW = 0.77$

(5) $\quad S_t^{ui} = -14.523 + \underset{(0.039)}{0.182}\ Y_t^{ui} + \underset{(0.195)}{0.249}\ S_{t-1}^{ui} \qquad R^2 = 0.879 \\ \qquad\qquad\qquad\qquad\qquad\qquad\qquad\qquad\qquad\qquad\qquad DW = 2.08$

(6) $\quad C_t^{ui} = 14.374 + \underset{(0.044)}{0.805}\ Y_t^{ui} \qquad\qquad\qquad\qquad \bar{R} = 0.988 \\ \qquad\qquad\qquad\qquad\qquad\qquad\qquad\qquad\qquad\qquad\qquad DW = 0.77$

(7) $\quad S^{ri} = -8.582 + \underset{(0.039)}{0.177}\ Y_t^{ri} + \underset{(0.198)}{0.253}\ S^{ri}_{t-1} \qquad \bar{R} = 0.878 \\ \qquad\qquad\qquad\qquad\qquad\qquad\qquad\qquad\qquad\qquad\qquad DW = 2.09$

(8) $\quad C_t^{ri} = 8.442 + \underset{(0.043)}{0.811}\ Y_t^{ri} \qquad\qquad\qquad\qquad \bar{R}^2 = 0.978 \\ \qquad\qquad\qquad\qquad\qquad\qquad\qquad\qquad\qquad\qquad\qquad DW = 0.77$

where S_t = current savings;

Y_t = current available income;

C_t = current consumption expenditure;

uh = urban households;

rh = rural households;

ui = urban individuals;

ri = rural individuals.

It is clear from equations (1)-(8) that savings per household and per head in both sectors do not depend only on current income but also on past saving. On the other hand, consumption per household and per head in both sectors depends mainly on current income. This implies that savings appear to be explained best by the permanent income hypothesis, while consumption expenditures appear to follow the Keynesian hypothesis.

3.   The choice of the appropriate
      saving/consumption relationship

Having estimated the consumption and savings functions, one now needs to define the relationship between savings and consumption. Two criteria will be applied in choosing this relation. The first is the shape of the function-linear or non-linear, which involves relatively more realistic assumptions regarding the saving behaviour of the households and individuals in the different expenditure brackets (specifically the difference in the saving behaviour of the poor and the rich households). The second criterion is that the form should meet the available data constraint of having a set of consumption expenditure of households and individuals (per expenditure brackets) for one year only, from which we should get our estimates of the households' saving. Two forms of function are ruled out according to the second criterion: the functions with an intercept,[6] and lagged functions. Applying these two criteria, the following saving/consumption relation has been chosen for our purpose:

(9) $S_{i,t} = \alpha\, C_{i,t}$

where S_i and C_i are saving per household or per head and consumption per household or per head in the i-th expenditure bracket; η is the elasticity of saving with respect to consumption expenditure, and t refers to the time period.[7]

Table 3.1: Distribution of household consumption expenditure and household available income (in percentages); original data and data adjusted for National Accounts, per household and per head - Egypt, 1974-75

Income concept	Consumption expenditure						Adjusted available income					
Recipient unit	Per household			Per person			Per household			Per person		
Area	Rural	Urban	Total	Rural	Urban	Total	Rural	Urban	Total	Rural	Urban	Total
Deciles:												
I	2.3	2.5	2.2	3.2	2.8	3.0	2.1	2.3	2.1	2.9	2.5	2.8
II	4.2	4.2	4.0	5.9	4.9	5.1	3.9	3.8	3.7	5.6	4.6	4.8
III	5.6	5.3	5.2	6.5	5.4	5.5	5.1	4.9	4.9	6.0	5.0	5.1
IV	6.6	6.3	6.2	7.1	6.1	6.4	6.1	5.8	5.8	6.6	5.6	5.9
V	7.3	7.3	7.9	7.9	7.2	7.2	7.2	6.7	6.8	7.3	6.6	6.7
VI	8.9	8.6	8.4	9.2	8.0	8.0	8.2	8.0	7.9	8.5	7.4	7.5
VII	10.3	10.2	10.2	10.2	9.8	10.1	9.6	9.5	9.5	9.5	9.1	9.4
VIII	12.1	12.1	12.1	12.0	11.5	11.4	11.4	11.3	11.3	11.2	10.8	10.7
IX	15.1	15.6	15.7	14.2	15.1	14.6	14.4	14.8	14.9	13.5	14.3	13.9
X	27.1	27.9	28.8	23.8	29.3	28.6	31.9	32.9	33.2	28.8	34.2	33.3
Gini index	0.35	0.36	0.37	0.28	0.35	0.34	0.39	0.40	0.40	0.32	0.39	0.38

The chosen non-linear form of the saving/consumption relation fulfils the two criteria. Regarding the first criterion, it implies that the saving/consumption ratio per household and per head (S/C) and the change in saving as compared to change in consumption (dS/dC) are positively related to the level of consumption, so that: $\eta > 1.$[8]   This means that the household and the individual with a relatively high level of consumption expenditure has a relatively higher level of savings.

4. Estimating savings and adjusted available income

The first task in this section is to estimate the elasticity of savings with respect to consumption expenditure (i.e. the coefficient η in equation (9)).   In fact, this elasticity is equal to the elasticity of savings with respect to income ($E_{s,y}$) divided by the elasticity of consumption with respect to income ($E_{c,y}$) so that $\eta = E_{s,y}/E_{c,y}.$ The latter two elasticities can be estimated from the functions (1) to (8) for households and persons in both urban and rural areas.   The savings elasticity in 1974/75 was estimated as the average of the short-run and the long-run elasticities in the two years, 1974 and 1975, while the consumption elasticity was estimated as the average of the calculated values for 1974 and 1975.[9]   The calculated values for η were:

> uh $= 4.04;$
>
> rh $= 3.53;$
>
> ui $= 3.62;$ and
>
> ri $= 3.54.$

The second step is to estimate the coefficient   of the saving/consumption relation (see equation (9)) subject to the constraints:

$$\sum_{i=1}^{N} S_i H_i = S \text{ and } \sum_{j=1}^{N} S_j P_j = S$$

for respectively the per household and the per head saving/consumption relations (i and j refer to respectively per household and per head income brackets; H and P to respectively households and individuals; and S to total savings from the National Accounts data).   The coefficients α can be calculated from the above constraints and equation (9).

It is worth making a few remarks on the estimates of savings in both urban and rural areas. First, the average savings in the low expenditure brackets is almost nil in both sectors. This corresponds with what one would expect, because at low levels of incomes all income will be directed to meet the consumption needs of the family. However, one should not exclude the possibility of some individual low income households with dissavings. Second, in all expenditure brackets, household savings are higher in the rural than in the urban sector. This can be explained by the fact that, generally, the spending opportunities are fewer in the rural sector than in the urban sector; for instance, the expenditure on rent, transportation and entertainment are significantly lower for the rural households than for the urban ones. Thus, having the same disposable income, the rural household (or individual) is expected to save more out of it and hence has lower consumption expenditure level than the urban household (or individual). By the same token, urban and rural households (individuals) belonging to the same consumption expenditure bracket probably belong to different disposable income brackets, with the rural households falling in a higher income bracket (and hence having higher savings) than the urban households.

5. Results

Having estimated the adjusted consumption expenditure and savings for households and individuals in both urban and rural areas, it is now possible to calculate the various distributions (see table 3.1).

Table 3.1 shows that the inequality of adjusted available income is more than 10 per cent higher than that of consumption expenditure. This is explained by two facts. First, income inequality is generally higher than expenditure inequality, and, secondly, the concentration of savings in the high-income classes adds further to inequality. It is also noteworthy that the per head distributions in rural areas are considerably less unequal than the per household distributions, while this is not the case in urban areas. Since there is no information available on the distribution of households by household size, it is not possible to provide an explanation for this difference.

Notes

[1] Central Agency of Public Mobilisation and Statistics (CAPMAS): Employment sample survey, 1974-75 (Cairo, 1977) (in Arabic).

[2] CAPMAS: Household budget sample survey in Egypt, 1974-75: The four-round combined results (Cairo, 1978) (in Arabic).

[3] For a review of the theoretical and empirical literature on saving in the two lines of thoughts, see R.F. Mikesell: "The nature of the savings function in developing countries: A survey of the theoretical and empirical literature", in Journal of Economic Literature (Nashville, Tennessee, American Economic Association), Mar. 1973, pp. 1-26.

[4] See, for example, the formulation of the saving and consumption functions according to the Friedman "permanent income hypothesis" which has been experimented within the Indian case by U.D.R. Choudbury: "Income, consumption and savings in urban and rural India", in Review of Income and Wealth, Mar. 1968, pp. 38-40 and pp. 47-48. See also Mikesell, op. cit., p. 3.

[5] Since our ultimate objective is to estimate disposable income, one may wonder why we do not use the estimated consumption functions to compute directly the available income corresponding to the household's and per head consumption expenditure in the different expenditure brackets. This cannot be done since the coefficients of the consumption function - no matter what its functional form is - are estimated by using C and Y of the average household or individual on the national level, which are higher than the levels of C and Y prevailing in almost half the expenditure brackets. Consequently, applying the estimated consumption function to estimate the disposable income of the households or individuals in the different expenditure brackets will give meaningless results. It implies dissaving for the consumption units in almost half the expenditure brackets (the bottom half, of course, which falls below the average national figures); moreover, the level of dissaving in the relatively low expenditure brackets is unreasonably high as compared to the household's and individual's consumption expenditure in those brackets.

[6] To estimate the intercept using average household's and individual's saving and consumption on the national level and then apply this intercept to estimate household's and individual's saving in the different expenditure bracket does give meaningless results; it gives dissaving for the households and individuals in almost half the expenditure brackets (see footnote 5 above).

[7] This chosen form of the saving/consumption relation may be written in linear form; it will take then a double-logarithmic form:

$$\log S_t = \log \alpha + \eta \log C_t$$

[8] Since, from equation (9), the S/C and the dS/dC ratios are as follows:

$$S/C = \alpha C^{\eta - 1} \quad \text{and} \quad dS/dC = \eta \alpha C^{\eta - 1}$$

Thus, if $\eta > 1$, then S/C and dS/dC increase with the increase of C.

9 For more information, see K. Korayem: The estimation of the disposable income distribution in Egypt (Geneva, ILO, 1982; mimeographed World Employment Programme research working paper; restricted), pp. 14-18.

4. FIJI (1977)

(S. Stavenuiter, ILO, Suva)

Summary

The Fijean income distribution estimates are based on the 1977 Household Income and Expenditure Survey (HIES)[1] and adjusted according to the totals of the 1977 Social Accounting Matrix (SAM). Given the lack of disaggregation in the Social Accounting Matrix, the income concept employed was "gross available income" which equals available income plus personal income tax and employees' contributions to social security. The study generated the distributions of gross available income per household and per head; in urban areas, settlements and villages.

1. Introduction

The 1977 Household Income and Expenditure Survey (HIES) is the first nation-wide household survey in Fiji of sufficient scope and coverage to permit a meaningful analysis of income distribution data. The nation-wide budget survey of 1965 covered only 734 households and later surveys were only conducted in urban areas. The 1977 HIES covered 2,554 households, 3 per cent of all urban households and 2.5 per cent of all rural households.

Data collection was spread over a 12-month period. A two-week daily system was used for recording details on daily expenditure, subsistence consumption and exchange of gifts, subsistence items being valued at prices prevailing in the nearest market. Expenditures of an irregular nature were recorded separately, using appropriate recall periods. Finally, detailed income data were collected, also applying appropriate recall periods for seasonal and irregular sources of income.

Undersampling of small households seems not to have been a problem with the 1977 HIES. In the survey sample, 2.3 per cent of households consisted of one person only, while the 1976 population census found 3.3 per cent one-person households. The average household size in the sample population was 5.8 persons, compared with 6.0 in the population census. Because these differences are marginal, no corrections for discrepancies with demographic aggregates appeared to be required.

The household concept applied in the HIES was the Fiji census definition: "those persons who usually eat together food prepared in the same kitchen and who together share the work and cost of providing the food". This adequately covers the definition of the 1980 World Population Census Programme.

The 1977 HIES data allow the construction of income distribution estimates according to almost any income concept. However, since National Accounts do not provide information on aggregate household available income the concept of gross household income had to be applied: household income before personal income tax and employees' social security payments, including subsistence consumption and subsistence gifts received (valued at prices prevailing in the nearest market), as well as the imputed rental value of owner-occupied and rent-free housing.[2]

2. Comparison with National Accounts

The Social Accounting Matrix (SAM)[3] constructed for Fiji 1977, contains 180 accounts. It implicitly reconciles the findings of the 1977 HIES with National Accounts aggregates by including them in a balanced and consistent framework. Of relevance to this exercise are the sub-matrices detailing factor payments and transfer payments to categories of households, as well as payments by production activities to factors of production. The factor payments to households are insufficiently disaggregated for a direct comparison with the sources of household income specified in the HIES. However, tracing back the origin of factor payments to production activities made it possible to produce a breakdown of household income by source comparable with the classification adopted in the household survey. It should be noted that the nature of the Social Accounting Matrix precludes a comparison of HIES net household income by source with the SAM-aggregates, as payments of direct taxes and of employees' contributions to social security by households cannot be related to the source of household income.

The 1977 HIES estimates the average annual household per head income at F$672. The estimated mid-year population in 1977 was F$596,000, giving an estimated aggregate household income of F$400,512,000. Total household incomes according to the 1977 SAM amounted to F$545,074,000, suggesting that the household survey underestimated household incomes by 26.5 per cent (see table 4.1).

Absolute and relative discrepancies between the aggregated survey results and the SAM aggregates appear to vary considerably by source of income. Business incomes appear to have been under-recorded in the survey by as much as 72 per cent, probably as a result of deliberate under-reporting by high income earners, but probably also because small businessmen may not have had an accurate knowledge of the magnitude of their irregular income. The apparent under-recording of income from sugar-cane growing by 50 per cent may be partly attributed to deliberate under-reporting, but is also partly a result of the fact that annual income data from farming collected

Table 4.1: Household incomes by source according to the 1977
Household Income and Expenditure Survey (HIES) and the
1977 Social Accounting Matrix (SAM), Fiji (F$'000)

Income source	HIES	SAM	SAM-HIES	% under-recording
Wages and salaries	227 184	250 812*	23 628	9.4
Business income	36 475	131 927	95 452	72.4
Sugar-cane growing	24 823	49 377	24 554	49.7
Other agriculture	13 811	13 420	- 391	- 2.9
Subsistence income	39 384	40 071	687	1.7
Capital income	8 727	7 659	- 1 068	-13.9
Imputed rent	37 817	29 000	- 8 817	-30.4
Transfer and other income	12 291	22 808	10 517	46.1
Gross household income	400 512	545 074	142 662	26.2

* The payment of wages and salaries is given in the SAM as
F$252.912 million, as the total wage bill includes employers'
contributions to social security. These have been excluded here for
reasons of comparability.

during the earlier stages of the survey referred mainly to income
earned in 1976, when both sugar-cane production and prices paid to
farmers were substantially lower than in 1977. The 46 per cent
under-recording of transfer and other income is fairly small in
absolute terms, and may be largely due to inadequate recall of
irregular sources of income. Though the survey's under-recording of
wage and salary incomes is rather modest in relative terms (9 per
cent), it is of the same absolute order of magnitude as that of income
from sugar-cane farming. Discrepancies in subsistence income and in
other agricultural income are insignificant.

Table 4.2: Distribution of gross available household income (in percentages); original data and data adjusted for National Accounts, per household and per head (Fiji, 1977)

Type of data	Original		Adjusted	
Income concept	I	II	I	II
Recipient unit	Household	Person	Household	Person
Deciles				
I	1.3	1.6	1.1	1.4
II	2.9	3.2	2.6	2.8
III	4.4	4.4	4.0	3.9
IV	5.6	5.9	4.8	5.4
V	6.9	6.5	6.0	6.0
VI	8.2	7.9	7.4	7.3
VII	9.9	9.2	9.4	8.8
VIII	12.6	11.7	11.5	11.1
IX	16.6	15.8	15.5	15.3
X	31.7	33.8	37.8	38.0
Gini index	0.42	0.43	0.47	0.46

I: gross available household income;
II: gross available household income per head.

The survey results in a higher estimate of capital income than that implied by the SAM. As capital income is usually underestimated rather than overestimated by household surveys, the HIES figure is probably a better estimate than the SAM figure. The same applies to the discrepancy in the estimates of the imputed rental value of owner-occupied and rent-free housing.

3. Nation-wide results

In accordance with Altimir's methodology,[4] all income sources were proportionally adjusted for under-reporting, while the household survey aggregates which were higher than National Accounts estimates (other agriculture, capital income and imputed rent) were not adjusted. Table 4.2 shows the results for both the per household and the per head[5] distribution.

The average household income in each decile is increased as a result of the adjustments made. The adjustments thus reduce the estimated incidence of poverty. On the other hand, measured inequality is increased, as after adjustment all deciles but the highest receive a smaller share of income. This shift in measured inequality is largely the result of the allocation pattern of business incomes, which are very unevenly distributed. Wages and salaries also are more unequally distributed over deciles of households than the unadjusted gross household incomes.

The adjustment led to an increase of the gini index from 0.42 for the original distribution to 0.47 for the adjusted distribution - a substantial increase of 5 percentage points.

4. Results for urban and rural areas

Similar decile income distribution tabulations of household and per head income broken down by income source as were computed for the nation-wide survey sample were also obtained for the subsamples of households living in urban areas, rural settlements and rural villages. The subdivision of rural households in two categories was prompted by the fact that Fiji's rural areas are characterised by two distinct modes of economic activity and social organisation. The "settlement" sector consists almost exclusively of farming households of Indian descent, primarily engaged in the production of cash crops. The "village" category comprises the inhabitants of ethnically Fijian villages, and is characterised by a heavy dependence on subsistence production and a more communal life-style.

For each source of household income of urban, settlement and village households aggregates have been estimated on the basis of the HIES. The under-recording of the four income sources for which the nation-wide distributions were adjusted are allocated proportionately to the urban, settlement and village categories in the bottom part of the table. The allocations increase the estimated average urban incomes by 50 per cent, average settlement incomes by 32 per cent and average village incomes by 11 per cent. Urban-rural income gaps increase substantially as a result of the adjustments, mainly because 94 per cent of the under-recorded part of business income is allocated to urban income earners.

Applying Altimir's methodology as described in section 3 produces the results for urban and rural areas (table 4.3).

The distribution of urban household incomes is most seriously affected by the adjustments. This is caused, first, by the fact that under-reporting of income was apparently more serious in urban than in rural areas, and, second, because the urban distribution had to be adjusted mainly for the under-recording of highly unequally distributed business incomes. Adjustments made the gini index rise from 0.42 to 0.48.

5. Conclusion

Adjustment for under-recording resulted in a higher degree of measured inequality for all eight sets of distribution data that were corrected. Table 4.4 summarises the changes in the estimates of the Gini indices resulting from the adjustments, the percentage increases in average income caused, as well as the original and adjusted urban-rural gaps in the form of average income indices (national average = 100).

The adjusted nation-wide and area distributions of per head income all show a greater degree of equality than the corresponding distributions of houshold incomes. However, the Lorenz curves for household and per head incomes intersect for the nation-wide, urban and settlement distribution, indicating that the distribution of per head incomes, though more equal, is at the same time more skewed.

While the adjustments cause average urban incomes to increase by as much as 50 per cent, settlement and village incomes are only increased by 32 per cent and 11 per cent respectively, resulting in wider observed income disparities between urban and rural areas, as well as between settlements on the one side and traditional Fijian villages on the other.

Table 4.3: Distribution of gross household available income and per head (in percentages); original data and data adjusted for National Accounts, urban areas, villages and settlements (Fiji, 1976)

Area	Urban areas				Settlements				Villages			
Type of data	Original		Adjusted		Original		Adjusted		Original		Adjusted	
Recipient unit*	I	II	I	II	I	II	I	II	I	II	I	II
Deciles												
I	1.1	1.5	1.0	1.6	1.0	1.8	2.2	2.8	2.2	2.8	2.2	2.7
II	3.3	3.3	3.3	2.9	3.0	3.6	2.7	3.4	3.5	3.8	3.3	3.6
III	4.5	4.5	3.7	4.0	4.9	4.3	4.6	4.5	4.5	5.1	4.3	4.9
IV	5.5	5.7	4.4	5.1	6.3	6.8	6.0	6.8	5.7	6.4	5.6	6.1
V	6.6	6.4	5.4	5.5	7.7	8.0	7.0	8.0	7.0	7.2	6.7	7.0
VI	7.9	7.8	7.2	7.0	9.2	8.7	9.1	8.8	8.6	8.6	8.3	8.4
VII	10.1	9.4	8.8	8.6	11.0	10.4	11.1	10.4	10.3	10.2	10.0	10.1
VIII	12.7	11.5	11.6	10.3	13.3	12.3	13.4	11.9	12.4	12.4	12.2	12.3
IX	16.7	17.8	15.6	16.2	16.6	15.7	16.4	15.0	16.6	16.0	16.8	15.9
X	31.7	32.1	38.9	38.8	27.0	27.8	29.0	29.5	29.3	27.5	30.6	29.0
Gini index	0.42	0.42	0.48	0.47	0.39	0.37	0.41	0.38	0.39	0.36	0.40	0.37

* I: gross household income per household;
  II: gross household income per head.

Table 4.4: Summary results of the adjustmments of the nation-wide, urban, settlement and rural distribution of household and per head gross incomes for discrepancies with Social Accounting Matrix aggregates (Fiji, 1977)

	Original gini index	Adjusted gini index	Increase in ave. income (%)	Original average income index	Adjusted average income index
Household income:					
Urban	0.42	0.48	49.8	127.9	138.4
Settlement	0.39	0.41	32.0	80.3	76.6
Village	0.39	0.40	10.9	73.3	58.7
Nation-wide	0.42	0.47	38.5	100.0	100.0
Per head income:					
Urban	0.42	0.47	49.8	140.3	151.8
Settlement	0.37	0.38	32.0	74.6	71.1
Village	0.36	0.37	10.9	72.3	57.9
Nation-wide	0.43	0.46	38.5	100.0	100.0

Notes

[1] Thus far, only a report on the survey methodology has been published: Bureau of Statistics: Household income and expenditure survey, 1977, Report 1: Survey methodology (Suva, 1981). The Bureau of Statistics kindly provided the special tabulations required for the present exercise.

[2] Exclusion of reported personal income tax and employees' contributions to social security would reduce the average reported household income by 10 per cent. Due to the progressive incidence of these two components, the distribution of unadjusted "net" household incomes is characterised by a gini coefficient of 0.401, as compared with a gini index of 0.425 for the distribution of "gross" household incomes.

[3] The Social Accounting Matrix (SAM) for Fiji in 1977 was estimated by a team from the British Overseas Development Agency; the methods and assumptions underlying the construction of the SAM, as well as the figures used in the present chapter, are taken from ODA: Report on the Fiji SAM mission, Feb.-Mar. 1980 (London, 1980; mimeographed).

[4] O. Altimir: Income distribution estimates from household surveys and population censuses in Latin America: An assessment of reliability (Washington, DC, World Bank, Development Research Centre, 1977; mimeographed).

[5] The distribution of household per head incomes was available only for deciles of households, ranked by household per head income. The deciles, therefore, contained different population shares, as the average household size was found to be smaller in the higher deciles and larger in the lower deciles. As a breakdown of income by source was only available for the household deciles, adjustments were made to this decile distribution.

5. FRANCE (1975)

(W. van Ginneken, ILO, Geneva)

Summary

The French income distribution estimates are based on a sample of the 1975 tax declaration forms. The incomes of each individual household have been supplemented by incomes (mainly transfers) which are not taxable. Various sources of income were made consistent with National Accounts totals. The income concept is household disposable income which equals household available income minus imputed rent of owner-occupied houses. The results include three types of income distribution: per household, per head and per equivalent unit.

1. The 1975 tax-survey data

About every five years INSEE[1] takes a sample of about 40,000 households from the tax declaration forms. This sample is representative of all households, whether they pay taxes or not. The income unit is the household, i.e. all persons who live in the same dwelling. The incomes of each individual household have been supplemented by incomes (mainly transfers) which are not taxable, such as pensions, family benefits and housing subsidies.[2] The concept of "disposable household income" which is used in the 1975 data is not exactly the same as the concept of "household available income" which is used for most other countries. In fact, "household disposable income" does not include imputed rent or owner-occupied houses. Since imputed rent normally rises proportionally with income the two concepts are not likely to show a great difference in inequality.

2. Consistency with National Accounts and population data

As is usually the case, the aggregated incomes of the survey underestimate the corresponding National Accounts totals. Table 5.1 provides an indication of this underestimation.

Table 5.1: Disposable income from the 1975 survey compared with data derived from the 1975 National Accounts (in millions of francs)

Sources of income	National Accounts[1] (1)	1975 survey[2] (2)	Ratio of 100* (2) to (1) (3)
Net wages and salaries	522 812	504 667	96.5
Entrepreneurial income from agriculture	49 187	14 412	29.3
Entrepreneurial income from non-agriculture	151 330	90 144	59.6
Property income	70 199	40 915	58.3
Transfer income*	170 653	145 242	85.1
Direct taxes	73 467	75 289	102.5
Disposable household income	890 704	720 091	80.8

* Excludes health benefits, work accident and unemployment benefits.

[1] See M.E. Martin: "Les disparités de revenu entre catégories sociales en 1975", in Economie et statistique (Paris, INSEE), No. 117, Dec. 1979, p. 27.

[2] Based on tables supplied by INSEE.

The table shows that, in particular, entrepreneurial income from agriculture is underestimated, but that the underestimation for all entrepreneurial income is about 50 per cent, which is comparable with what is found for other countries. The underestimation percentages for other sources of income is also consistent with those found for other countries. The correction factors for the various sources of income are taken from column (3). This means that all income sources (except for property income) are multiplied by the reciprocal of the ratios shown in column (3). In the case of property income we allocated the underestimated part (i.e. 70,199-40,915) to the highest quintile of households, in proportion to their incomes.

Table 5.2: Distribution of household disposable income (in percentages), per household, per head and per equivalent unit; original data and data adjusted with National Accounts (France, 1975)

Type of data	Unadjusted			Adjusted		
Income concept*	I	II	III	I	II	III
Recipient unit	Household	Person	Person	Household	Person	Person
	(1)	(2)	(3)	(4)	(5)	(6)
Deciles						
I	1.7	2.6	2.8	1.8	3.2	3.4
II	3.5	4.5	4.7	3.5	4.7	5.0
III	4.8	5.3	5.8	4.9	5.3	5.7
IV	6.3	6.3	6.6	6.2	6.0	6.4
V	7.7	7.3	7.7	7.4	6.9	7.2
VI	9.1	8.7	8.8	8.6	8.2	8.2
VII	10.7	10.2	10.2	10.0	9.5	9.6
VIII	12.7	12.6	12.5	11.8	11.9	11.6
IX	15.8	16.3	16.1	15.3	16.0	15.9
X	27.7	26.2	24.8	30.5	28.2	26.9
Gini index	0.38	0.34	0.32	0.39	0.35	0.33

* I: household disposable income;
 II: household disposable income per head;
III: household disposable income per equivalent unit.

Note: The decile distributions are calculated on the basis of tables cross-classifying households by household disposable income (in deciles) and household size (eight groups).

There does not seem to be any reason to adjust the household size distribution because the distribution shown by the survey is almost similar to that of the 1975 population census.[3]

4. Results

Table 5.2 shows the main results for France. The estimates are based on tables which cross-classify households by disposable income (in deciles) and household size (1, 2, 3, 4, 5, 6, 7, 8+) (see appendix). The lack of data on household food expenditure did not allow us to estimate the economies-of-scale factor as we did for other countries. According to a French convention, we have attributed one consumption unit to the head of household, 0.7 to persons older than 13 years, and 0.5 to children less than 14 years old.

It was, first, to be expected that the household distribution for adjusted income (column (4) is more unequal than that for unadjusted income (column (1). This is due to the fact that non-agricultural entrepreneurial income and income from property are concentrated in the highest decile. This difference is less marked for the per head and per equivalent distributions. It can, secondly, be noted that the per head and per equivalent distributions are less unequal than the per household distribution.

Notes

[1] See A. Villeneuve: "Les revenus primaires des ménages en 1975", in Economie et statistique (Paris, INSEE), No. 103, Sep. 1978, pp. 59-72.

[2] See M.E. Martin: "Les disparités de revenu entre catégories sociales en 1975", in Economie et statistique, No. 117, Dec. 1979, pp. 23-35.

[3] INSEE: Principaux résultats du recensement de 1975, Les Collections de l'INSEE, Démographie et emploi, D.52 (Paris, 1977), p. 160.

Appendix 5.1: Distribution of households by deciles of disposable household income and by household size (France, 1975)

Deciles (households)	Household size								Total income	Average
	(1)	(2)	(3)	(4)	(5)	(6)	(7)	(8)		
I	1 337 348	264 672	99 332	42 259	18 910	8 160	1 580	1 583	1 773 774	6 916
II	800 925	697 800	132 257	83 079	39 199	12 725	3 493	1 681	1 771 159	14 076
III	637 928	706 451	213 163	128 547	49 370	25 349	8 688	5 629	1 775 125	19 655
IV	411 582	637 007	369 858	205 801	88 965	35 185	15 248	7 056	1 770 702	25 491
V	268 872	570 970	408 022	293 262	143 727	51 952	28 282	10 979	1 776 066	31 155
VI	153 691	487 698	390 519	394 376	201 641	82 051	40 728	24 253	1 775 227	36 972
VII	121 071	434 815	432 549	354 175	211 652	109 642	56 031	47 983	1 767 918	43 517
VIII	76 701	418 731	476 139	352 897	217 908	111 678	52 402	66 389	1 772 845	51 618
IX	66 526	365 432	486 687	411 067	212 049	128 757	49 273	52 542	1 772 333	64 203
X	53 064	350 947	391 406	462 637	268 639	125 899	46 514	73 305	1 772 411	112 649
Total	3 927 778	4 934 523	3 399 832	2 728 100	1 452 060	691 398	302 239	291 670	17 727 530	40 620
Average income (FF/gross year)	19 737	36 932	47 043	52 808	55 803	57 554	55 650	64 074	40 620	

Source: INSEE.

6. FEDERAL REPUBLIC OF GERMANY (1974)

(W. van Ginneken, ILO, Geneva)

Summary

The German income distribution estimates are based on 1974 figures from the German Institute for Economic Research (DIW) and which were already adjusted for inconsistencies with National Accounts. The income concept is household available income. Three types of income distribution estimates were generated: per household, per head and per equivalent unit.

1. Introduction

There are two data sets which include income distribution data which are adjusted for inconsistencies with National Accounts and population censuses. The first is produced by the German Institute for Economic Research (Berlin). The main findings are published in two monographs[1] and are regularly updated in the weekly review[2] of the Institute. The second is the so-called IMDAF (integrated micro-data file) of Frankfurt University.[3]

The difference between the two is that the IMDAF set readjusts household observations as measured in the 1962/63 and 1969 household income and expenditure surveys, while the DIW set is based on a model which includes information from various sources. The income concepts used by both data sets are not completely comparable. The DIW data set uses the National Accounts definition of available private household income (i.e. including imputed rent, but after tax, social security contributions and social transfers), while the IMDAF data include some components such as voluntary social security contributions of the self-employed.[4] There is also some difference between the household concepts used by both data sets. The IMDAF data set includes patients and/or members of institutions as one-person households as well as subletters or workers who live in the same dwelling but who do not share incomes or expenditures.

In this chapter we shall base our income estimates on the DIW data set. The main reason for this is that this set permits long-term comparisons of income inequality (between 1955 and 1978). Moreover, the DIW data are adjusted for inconsistencies with disposable household income of the National Accounts which permits international comparisons.

2. Distribution of income per household,
   per equivalent adult and per head (1974)

The data published by DIW are primarily based on income and
expenditure surveys (1962, 1968/69, 1973), supplemented by data from
housing surveys, the micro-census and income tax records. The data
are then made consistent with disposable private household income from
the National Accounts. The relation with National Accounts is made
through the link with individual income earners. Data on households,
population and income earners are taken from population censuses,
supplemented by the annual data from the micro-census.

Given the distribution of disposable private household income by
household size, and the expenditure pattern per income class, it is
possible to estimate the distributions of income per household, per
head and per equivalent unit. The so-called "economies-of-scale"
factor was estimated from the following two double-log food
expenditure functions:

$$\log F = 1.995 + \underset{(0.008)}{0.611} \log Y + \underset{(0.009)}{0.246} \log N \qquad R^2 = 0.99 \\ e = 0.632$$

$$\log (F/N) = 2.068 + \underset{(0.007)}{0.601} \log (Y/N) - \underset{(0.008)}{0.127} \log N \qquad R^2 = 0.99 \\ e = 0.682$$

All coefficients are highly significant and the
economies-of-scale factor amounts to 0.632. With the formula $\log Y =$
$0.632 \log N$, one can calculate the equivalent scales for various
household sizes.

Household size	Our estimate	Beckerman[5]	
1	100	100	Single adult
2	155	161	Couple
3	200	197	Couple + 1 child
4	240	231	Couple + 2 children
5	277	266	Couple + 3 children
6	310	319	Couple + 4 children or more

These equivalent scales are well comparable with those based on
the British official supplementary benefit scale rates and employed by
Beckerman in a study comparing poverty estimates in various OECD
countries.[5]

The original data are classified according to 20 income classes
and 5 household sizes (1, 2, 3, 4, 5+). On this basis it is well
feasible to give an accurate estimate of the decile distribution and
the gini index for the distribution of income per household and per
head and per equivalent unit (see table 6.1).

Table 6.1: Distribution of adjusted available household income (in percentages): per household, per head and per equivalent unit (Federal Republic of Germany, 1974)

Income concept*	I	II	III	I (1978)
Recipient unit	Household	Person	Person	Household
Deciles				
I	2.9	3.6	3.7	2.3
II	4.0	4.8	5.0	4.0
III	5.0	5.7	5.9	5.3
IV	6.0	6.7	6.7	6.5
V	7.1	7.4	7.6	7.6
VI	8.3	8.7	8.7	8.8
VII	9.9	9.9	10.0	10.4
VIII	12.0	11.6	11.8	12.3
IX	16.0	14.8	14.5	15.4
X	28.8	26.8	26.0	27.4
Gini index	0.37	0.32	0.31	0.36

* I: household available income;
 II: household available income per head;
III: household available income per equivalent unit.

As expected, the household incomes are more unequally distributed than per head income. This is so since the per head concept implies an averaging out of income differences. The distribution of income per equivalent unit is very similar to that of the per head distribution.

Schmaus[6] demonstrates with the IMDAF data set that the gini index of net income per head is considerably higher than that per equivalent unit. In his case, the distribution per equivalent unit is more correctly estimated, because the IMDAF data set permits reclassification of the individual household data into per equivalent unit income classes. The difference is mainly due to his detailed equivalent scales which allocate weights to age and sex groups. In addition, he accepts the equivalent adult as the welfare unit. For 1962/63 he finds that the gini indices for inequality of net incomes per household, per head and per equivalent unit are respectively 0.36, 0.32 and 0.29 and for 1969 respectively 0.35, 0.32 and 0.29.

Notes

[1] G. Göseke and K.-D. Bedau: Verteilung und Schichtung der Einkommen der privaten Haushalte in der Bundesrepublik Deutschland 1950 bis 1975 (Distribution and classification of private household incomes in the Federal Republic of Germany, 1950 to 1975) (Berlin, Deutsches Institut für Wirtschaftsforschung, 1974); idem: Einkommens- und Verbrauchsschichtung für die grösseren Verwendungsbereiche des privaten Verbrauchs und die privaten Ersparnisse in der Bundesrepublik Deutschland 1955 bis 1974 (Classification of income and expenditure for major private expenditure items and private savings in the Federal Republic of Germany, 1955 to 1974) (Berlin, Deutsches Institut für Wirtschaftsforschung, 1978).

[2] See for example, Wochenbericht (Berlin, Deutsches Institut für Wirtschaftsforschung), 15 Nov. 1979, pp. 467-478.

[3] K. Kortman: "Die Generierung einer geschlossenen Mikrodatenbasis für die Bundesrepublik Deutschland" (The generation of a closed micro-data base for the Federal Republic of Germany), in H.J. Krupp and W. Glatzer (eds.): Umveteilung im Sozialstaat (Redistribution in the welfare state) (Frankfurt, Campus Verlag, 1978), pp. 193-236.

[4] See G. Schmaus: "Personelle Einkommensverteilung im Vergleich 1962/63 und 1969" (Personal income distribution comparison between 1962/63 and 1969), in Krupp and Glatzer (eds.), op. cit., p. 77.

[5] W. Beckerman et al.: Poverty and the impact of income maintenance programmes (Geneva, ILO, 1979), p. 28.

[6] Schmaus, op. cit.

7. INDIA (1975-76)

(B. Rao, World Bank, Jakarta)

Summary

The Indian estimates are based on the 1975-76 Household Survey carried out by the National Council of Applied Economic Research (NCAER).   The income concept used in this survey is gross household available income, i.e. before taxes and contributions to social security.   It was not possible to adjust the income data for inconsistencies with National Accounts.   However, the population data were adjusted because the survey undercounted the number of households and did not take into account about 600,000 "homeless" households. As a result, 15 per cent of National Accounts remained unaccounted for.   Various types of income distribution estimates were generated: per household and per head, both in rural and in urban areas.

1.   Data sources

The source of data on income distribution in India was the periodic All India Household Survey conducted by the National Council of Applied Economic Research (NCAER).   The latest NCAER survey was for 1975-76.

Other income distribution estimates have been derived by combining various estimates of savings and distributions of consumption expenditures;   these have been gathered primarily through the national sample surveys.[1] These data were not used in this chapter.

2.   Brief description of the 1975-76 survey

The 1975-76 survey was conducted at the request of the Ministry of Finance and was designed to gather information on the distribution of household income, wealth and savings.   The survey covered all India except for a few small and inaccessible areas.   Of the total population of 548 million (1971 census count), only 1.2 million lived in the excluded areas.   The survey covered all private households, except for the population in institutions and the homeless population;   these groups numbered 4.6 million, or about 0.85 per cent of the total population.   The survey sample covered 5,125 households out of an estimated total of 100 million households.   The survey used the 12-month period, July 1975 to June 1976, as the reference period; it coincided with the agricultural year.

A household was defined as including all persons related by blood, marriage or adoption who had lived together for at least six months during the reference period and shared a common kitchen. It included single-person as well as multi-person households.

Household income was defined as the sum of earnings of all members from self-employment, employment, assets, transfers and imputations. Income referred to gross income (before payment of income taxes). Produce consumed by the producer was valued at market values. Employers' contributions to provident funds were included under wages and salaries. Income in kind and imputed rents for owner-occupied dwellings were included in total income. With respect to transfers, only regular transfers were included; these covered remittances and pensions.

3. Evaluation of the 1975-76 survey

Although the original survey sample included 5,602 households, income data were collected from only 5,125 households. Thus, the overall non-enumeration rate (include non-response) was 8.5 per cent. The urban non-enumeration rate was 11.1 per cent, as compared with 6.6 per cent for rural areas.

The survey estimated the total number of households to be 98.6 million, as compared with the census projected figure of 110.8 million as of 1 January 1976. Thus the 1975-76 survey appears to have under-enumerated households by about 11 per cent. The average household size reported in the survey was 5.97, as compared with the 1971 census estimate of 5.44 persons per household. As a result, the survey estimate of total population (589 million) was lower by only 1.9 per cent as compared with the official population figure (600 million).

A comparison of total household income as estimated from the survey (Rs.451,000 million) and as derived from the National Accounts data and governmental financial statistics (Rs.600,000 million) showed that the survey underestimated household income by about 25 per cent.

4. Derivation of income distribution

The survey data on income distribution were adjusted in two ways. First, the number of households in each income class was increased pro-rata to 110.2 million households, instead of using the 98.6 million provided by the survey. Second, the 0.6 million homeless households were added to the lowest income class, on the assumption that the "homeless" belong to the lowest income group. The above adjustments were made for rural and urban areas separately. The adjusted number of total households was 86.4 million in rural areas and 24.4 million in urban areas.

Table 7.1: Distribution of adjusted gross household income by households; (in percentages) in deciles (India, 1975-76)

Deciles (households)	Rural	Urban	Total country
I	2.7	2.4	2.5
II	4.6	3.6	3.4
III	4.7	4.2	4.5
IV	5.1	5.6	5.8
V	7.5	6.3	6.4
VI	7.6	7.6	7.5
VII	9.9	9.3	9.0
VIII	11.5	11.8	11.5
IX	15.0	15.8	15.8
X	31.4	33.4	33.6
Gini index	0.39	0.43	0.42

The total household income based on the adjusted survey data worked out to be 12.2 per cent higher than that based on the original survey data, but was still only 85 per cent of the expected total income of Rs.600,000 million in 1975-76. It was not possible to make any sensible assumption about how to adjust for the remaining 15 per cent of unaccounted income.

Table 7.1 gives income distribution by deciles of households and the gini index for rural and urban areas and the nation as a whole.

Table 7.2: Distribution of gross household income (in percentages)
per household and per capita. India, 1975-76

Income concept	Gross household income			Gross income per capita		
Recipient unit	Households			Person		
Area	Rural	Urban	Total country	Rural	Urban	Total country
Lowest 20%	7.3	6.0	7.0	8.7	6.9	7.5
Lowest 40%	17.1	15.8	16.2	20.2	16.9	18.5
Top 20%	46.4	49.2	49.4	42.4	48.8	46.5
Top 10%	31.4	33.4	33.6	27.6	34.1	31.4
Gini index	0.39	0.42	0.42	0.34	0.42	0.38

The NCAER report provides data on the distribution of population
by per head household income. These estimates are derived by
reclassifying the household members according to per head household
income, thus eliminating the effects of household size on the pattern
of income distribution. The data are given in terms of
percentages. Table 7.2 summarises the inequality measures for the
per head and household income distributions for rural, urban and
combined areas of India.

5. Concluding remarks

The pattern of household income distribution for India as a whole generally follows that of the urban areas, revealing more inequality than in the rural areas.

Despite some limitations, including under-enumeration of total households in the country, the 1975-76 survey had comprehensive geographical and income coverage and was based on generally sound concepts and definitions. Therefore the adjusted survey data can reasonably be assumed to reflect the actual pattern of income distribution in the country.

Note

[1] Data on the distribution of consumption expenditures are available from the National Sample Survey Organisation's (NSSO) periodic surveys. The NSSO started survey operations in 1950. The first detailed published report on consumer expenditures was for 1952.

Appendix 7.1: Distribution of households by total household income classes; urban and rural areas, total country (India, 1975-76)

Annual income class (Rs.)	Rural		Urban		All India	
	Mean income (Rs.)	Percentage of house-holds	Mean income (Rs.)	Percentage of house-holds	Mean income (Rs.)	Percentage of house-holds
1 200 and below	922	8.3	874	1.3	920	6.8
1 201- 2 400	1 804	29.8	1 864	11.6	1 810	25.9
2 401- 3 600	2 944	24.2	2 958	18.1	2 946	22.9
3 601- 4 800	4 112	14.6	4 113	16.3	4 112	15.0
4 801- 6 000	5 339	9.2	5 337	13.8	5 339	10.2
6 001- 7 500	6 679	5.0	6 752	10.1	6 705	6.1
7 501-10 000	8 664	3.9	8 512	11.2	8 597	5.5
10 001-15 000	12 127	3.0	12 014	8.6	12 077	4.2
15 001-20 000	16 906	1.0	17 232	4.2	17 077	1.7
20 001-25 000	22 033	0.5	22 453	2.1	22 258	0.8
25 001-30 000	27 511	0.3	27 137	1.2	27 298	0.5
over 30 000	46 013	0.2	47 371	1.5	46 926	0.5
All classes	3 897	100.0	7 074	100.0	4 579	100.0
No. of house-holds (million)		(77.4)		(21.2)		(98.6)

Source: NCAER: Survey for 1975-76.

8. ISLAMIC REPUBLIC OF IRAN (1973-74)

(F. Mehran, ILO, Geneva)

Summary

The estimates for the Islamic Republic of Iran are based on the 1973-74 rural and urban household budget surveys. The survey data on expenditures were adjusted to the National Account estimates and the results were added to estimates of household savings to obtain the adjusted distribution of household income. The study generated the distributions of household available income per household and per head.

The basic data used in this chapter are the household consumption expenditure estimates cross-classified by household size and income class, as published by the National Statistical Centre in the twin publications: Results of the rural household budget survey, 1352 and Results of the urban household budget survey, 1352. (The period between March 1973 and March 1974 corresponds to the Iranian calendar year 1352.)

These household budget surveys were conducted during the first seven months of the year 1352 and covered all private households in urban and rural areas, thus excluding collective households and the non-settled population (tribal and mobile households).

The net sample size was 9,371 households in the urban survey, covering 47,980 persons, and 9,361 households in the rural survey, covering 48,519 persons in 4,340 villages.

A two-stage stratified sampling design was used in both the urban and the rural surveys. In the first stage, in the urban survey, the population census tracts for the year 1345 (each tract containing about 1,000 households) were sampled, and in the second stage the households within the sampled census tracts were selected. In the rural survey, the first-stage sampling units were villages (localities with more than 5,000 inhabitants according to the 1345 population census) and the second-stage sampling units were households within the sampled villages.

The first-stage stratification criterion was city-size in the urban survey, measured in terms of number of inhabitants, and village-size in the rural survey, measured in terms of number of households. No stratification was used at the second stage of the sampling scheme in both surveys.

The household was defined on the basis of cohabitation and joint expenditure budget. The sampled households were interviewed by personal visits, and in certain cases repeated visits were made in order to make direct measurements of the quantity of consumption of certain food items. Where information was obtained on the basis of recall, the reference period was one day for food items, one month for non-food items, one month and 12 months for income.

1.   Adjustment to census population data

For the purpose of this study the survey population estimates were adjusted to estimates based on the population censuses. The method of adjustment involved two major steps: estimation of aggregate population level and number of private settled households in the year 1352 for benchmark purposes; and the corresponding estimation of the 1352 household size distribution.

The population data necessary for adjustment purposes were aligned to the number of private-settled households in the year 1352 with breakdown by urban and rural components. These were derived according to the following two-step procedures:

-   starting from the official total population figure for 1352,[1] the distribution of the population in private settled, mobile and tribal, and collective households were estimated using a weighted average of the corresponding distributions obtained from the 1345 and 1355 population censuses;[2]

-   the resulting estimate of the population in private-settled households were divided into urban and rural components on the basis of the urban-rural growth difference method.[3]

The number of households in private settled, mobile and tribal, and collective households in urban and rural areas were derived on the basis of estimates of the average household size in each category, estimated using a weighted average of the corresponding figures obtained from the 1345 and 1355 population censuses.

By way of evaluation of this method, the benchmark estimates were compared with the results of the 1350 demographic survey of urban and rural-settled population. It was found that the 1352 estimates tended to overstate the urban-settled population in relation to the rural-settled population by about 1 per cent.

Further, household size distribution obtained from the survey was adjusted to a modified version of the census household size distribution, separately for the urban and the rural population. The modification was needed in order to extrapolate the 1355 census distribution back to 1352, the year of the survey. The resulting adjusted distribution indicated that the number of smaller households were under-reported in the urban survey in relation to the census. However, no similar pattern emerged from the rural results.

The benchmark estimates of the percentage distribution of private settled households by household size in urban and rural areas, combined with the benchmark estimates of the number of such households, were then used to adjust proportionally the original survey household distribution data.

2. Adjustment to National Accounts

The survey data on expenditures were adjusted to the National Account estimates and the results were added to estimates of household savings to obtain the adjusted distribution of household income.

(a) Adjustment of the expenditure data. The adjustment procedure was performed for food and non-food items separately:

(i) food expenditure: detailed information were available on private consumption expenditure (on 34 items of expenditure) from the National Account estimates developed in the context of constructing a 59-sector input-output matrix for 1352.[4] For the purpose of the present chapter the National Accounts estimates were aggregated into 11 broad categories of food items and used, after minor modifications for tribal, mobile and collective households, as a benchmark for adjusting the survey data. The results are shown in table 8.1. It can be observed that the items of large discrepancies are other beverages, fruits, sugar, tea and coffee;

(ii) non-food expenditures: similar detailed information on non-food expenditures were not readily available from the 1352 National Accounts. The survey expenditure data on non-food items were therefore adjusted residually on the basis of the assumption that the ratio of adjusted food expenditure to total expenditure is equal to the corresponding ratio of unadjusted food expenditure to total expenditure[5] (see table 8.1).

(b) Estimation of household saving. A saving function was estimated using results obtained from a previous study on income inequality.[6] The saving function which incorporates household size was specified according to the following relationship:

$$S = \beta (I - \mu) \tag{1}$$

where S is household saving, I is household available income, μ is a parameter representing a fixed income level for which saving is zero and β is the unknown average propensity to save from an income in excess of the minimum income level.

Table 8.1: Aggregated household income as calculated from the 1352 (1973-74) survey and the corresponding estimated National Accounts totals (in millions of rials)

	Survey			National Accounts[1]	Ratio
	Urban (1)	Rural (2)	Total (3)	(4)	100* (3):(4)
Food expenditures[2]	160 474	143 924	304 398	349 628	87.1
Cereals	42 542	54 254	96 796	101 545	95.3
Meat	33 933	23 631	57 564	63 261	91.0
Dairy	24 186	25 176	49 362	54 174	91.1
Fruits	17 117	5 996	23 113	35 483	65.1
Vegetables	14 019	9 646	23 665	28 376	83.4
Sugar	7 268	10 465	17 733	20 184	87.9
Tea and coffee	4 980	6 905	11 885	15 122	78.6
Other beverages	764	51	815	13 272	6.1
Tobacco	6 588	5 827	12 415	14 551	85.3
Misc.	1 822	1 002	2 824	3 661	77.1
Non-food expenditures	244 357	82 227	326 584	512 213	63.8
Saving	-	-	-	(214 059)	-
Household income	-	-	-	1 075 900	-

[1] Slightly modified for tribal and collective households.

[2] Including pre-cooked and food consumed outside home.

Table 8.2: Percentage distribution of household available income per household and per head; adjusted and unadjusted data, Islamic Republic of Iran, 1352 (1973-74)

Decile	Original unadjusted distribution		Adjusted distribution	
	Per household	Per person	Per household	Per person
I	1.8	2.5	1.4	2.3
II	3.0	3.6	2.4	3.3
III	4.1	4.4	3.3	4.1
IV	5.0	5.2	4.2	4.9
V	6.5	6.1	5.6	5.8
VI	7.2	7.3	6.5	6.9
VII	9.0	8.7	8.3	8.3
VIII	11.3	11.1	10.9	10.8
IX	16.0	15.1	15.8	14.9
X	36.3	36.2	41.7	38.8
Gini index	0.46	0.44	0.52	0.47

The minimum income level was assumed to be different in rural and urban areas and to vary according to household size following the relationship:

$$\mu = \mu_o \, n^\theta$$

where μ_o^θ is the per head minimum income level for an average-size household, n is the household size and θ is a predetermined index of economies of scale set at $\theta = 0.7$.

Using regression techniques the saving function (1) was estimated for urban and rural households separately. The estimated values of the parameters of the saving functions with corresponding value of the R^2 coefficient are tabulated below:

	Urban	Rural
β	0.27	0.26
μ_o	16 722 rials	13 756 rials
R^2	0.988	0.977

Applying the saving function (rewritten as a function of expenditure) to the adjusted expenditure data derived earlier leads to an estimated aggregate household saving of 214,059 million rials or 19.9 per cent of aggregate household income (see table 8.1).

3. Results

The final results of this study are two income distributions, which were derived by adding the adjusted household expenditure and the estimated household saving and ordering the resulting adjusted household income in two ways: one based on ordering households according to adjusted household (available) income and the other based on ordering persons (individual members of the household) according to adjusted per head household (available) income. The two adjusted distributions in the form of deciles are shown in table 8.2 together with the corresponding unadjusted distributions based on the original data.

Notes

[1] Statistical Centre: Statistical Yearbook, 1356 (in Farsi) (Teheran, 1977), p. 33.

[2] idem: National census of population and housing, 1966, Publications No. 168 and 172 (Teheran, 1969); idem: National census of population and housing, November 1976, based on 5 per cent sample, total country (Teheran).

[3] United Nations: Methods for projections of urban and rural populations, Manuals on Methods of Estimating Population, Manual VIII (New York, United Nations, 1974; Sales No. E.74.XIII.3), pp. 25-31.

[4] Statistical Centre: Preliminary report on National Accounts of Iran (1350-1353), Series No. 1 (Teheran, Department of Financial Statistics and National Accounts, Apr. 1977), pp. 35-36.

[5] The total private consumption expenditure is taken for the total household consumption expenditure. Plan and Budget Organisation: Economic trends of Iran (Teheran, 5th ed., Mar. 1978), p. 128.

[6] F. Mehran: Income distribution in Iran: The statistics of inequality (Geneva, ILO, 1978; mimeographed World Employment Programme research working paper; restricted), p. 21.

9. IRELAND (1973)

(W. van Ginneken, ILO, Geneva)

Summary

The Irish income distribution estimates are based on the 1973 Household Budget Survey.[1] The income concept used by the survey is household disposable income which does not include imputed rent of owner-occupied houses. Each type of income - as measured by the survey - was adjusted to the corresponding National Accounts totals. The chapter generated the distributions of household disposable income per household, per head and per equivalent unit.

1. The 1973 household survey

The 1973 household budget survey covered a random representative sample of 7,748 urban and rural private households throughout the country. The sample was designed so that the total number of approximately 8,000 co-operating households sought from the survey were proportionally distributed as closely as possible on a regional basis. To allow for non-response, independent samples of 28 original and 28 substitute households were randomly selected in each survey area. Household interviewers canvassed the co-operation of all 28 original sample households and systematically approached the substitute households, until the co-operation of the specified quota of 28 households was realised. The actual number of households for which satisfactorily completed returns were actually obtained in individual areas was sometimes less than the required quota of 28. The household analysis based on the 1971 census of population was used to give the true distribution of households on the basis of location, household size, and social group of the head of the household. The actual distribution of the 7,748 sample households over the cells was obtained from the survey data. For a particular cell, the appropriate weighting factor was the ratio between the proportion of population households to the proportion of sample households in the cell.

The basic sampling unit is the household, which is defined as a single person or group of people who regularly reside together in the same accommodation and share the same catering arrangements. The household members defined in this fashion are not necessarily related by blood or by marriage. Thus, resident domestic servants and boarders are included. This household concept is similar to the housekeeping concept of the United Nations guide-lines. The latter concept, however, specifically requires that the members of the unit should make joint provisions for food and other essentials of living.

Table 9.1: Disposable income from the 1973 survey compared with data
from 1973 National Accounts (in millions of punts)

Source of income	1973 survey (1)	National Accounts (2)	100* (1):(2) = (3)
Wages and salaries[1]	976.9	1 349.9	72.3
Self-employed income (non-farm)	107.8	160.5	67.2
Self-employed income (farm)	282.3	363.1	77.7
Capital income[2]	28.1	186.9	15.0
State transfers	163.2	334.9	48.7
Taxes on income and wealth (including employees' social security contributions)	158.8	291.7	54.4
Disposable household income[1]	1 399.5	2 103.6	66.5

[1] Excluding social security contributions from employers.

[2] Does not include imputed rent for owner-occupied houses.

The income concept used for classification is household
disposable income, which includes wages and salaries of employees,
income from self-employment (farming and non-farming), retirement
pensions, investment income, property income, own garden/farm produce,
other direct income and state transfer payments (children's allowance,
pensions, unemployment benefits and education grants) after deduction
of income tax and social security contributions. This concept
differs from the concept of household available income in that it
excludes imputed rent from owner-occupied housing.

2. Consistency with population data
and National Accounts

Since (as was shown in the first section) the survey data were
weighed with factors derived from the 1971 Population Census, there is
no need to adjust distribution of households by household size.

Table 9.2: Estimates of double-log food expenditure functions
(Ireland, 1973)

				No. of observa-tions (weighted)
Log F	$= a$	$+ b \log Y$	$+ c \log N \quad R^2 \quad e$	
	1.355	0.092	0.712	
	(0.259)*	(0.091)	(0.071) 0.95 0.784	16
Log (F/N)	$= a$	$+ b \log (Y/N)$	$- t \log N \quad R^2$	
	1.355	0.092	0.196	
	(0.259)	(0.091)	(0.104) 0.76 0.784	16

* Figures in brackets are standard deviations.

Note: F = household expenditure on food;
Y = household disposable income (adjusted);
N = household size.

On the basis of National Accounts data[1] an attempt was made to compare the survey aggregates with the corresponding National Accounts totals (see table 9.1). This shows that the underestimation of the various income sources is fairly high, in particular for capital income.

3. Results

After adjustment of the income data, it is possible to estimate the economics-of-scale factor on the basis of double log food expenditure functions (see table 9.2).

Both estimates lead to the same value for the economies-of-scale factor (0.784), which was subsequently used to calculate household disposable income per equivalent unit. Table 9.3 shows the main results.

Table 9.3: Distribution of household disposable income (in percentages); original data and data adjusted for National Accounts, per household, per head and per equivalent unit (Ireland, 1973)

Type of data	Original			Adjusted		
Income concept*	I	II	III	I	II	III
Recipient unit	Household (1)	Person (2)	Person (3)	Household (4)	Person (5)	Person (6)
Deciles						
I	2.0	3.3	3.4	2.5	3.5	4.0
II	3.6	5.2	5.9	4.7	5.5	5.8
III	4.7	6.4	6.4	5.3	6.2	6.6
IV	7.7	6.7	6.9	7.8	6.5	7.6
V	8.2	7.8	8.1	8.2	8.1	8.0
VI	8.5	8.9	8.5	8.4	9.4	8.4
VII	10.7	10.2	10.4	10.4	10.2	9.9
VIII	14.1	11.5	12.9	13.3	10.9	12.2
IX	14.6	15.6	14.4	14.3	14.8	14.4
X	25.9	24.2	23.2	25.1	24.9	23.1
Gini index	0.35	0.30	0.28	0.32	0.29	0.27

* I: household disposable income;
II: household disposable income per head;
III: household disposable income per equivalent unit.

Note: The decile distributions are calculated on the basis of tables cross-classifying households by household disposable income (four classes) and household size (four classes).

It is unusual to find that the adjusted income distribution is somewhat less unequal than the original income distribution.

It was not possible to calculate the transition matrices, because the available tables include only 16 cells (see Appendix 9.1). This relatively low number of cells probably results from the fact that "measured" inequality - as shown in table 9.3 - underestimates "true" inequality to some extent.

Notes

1 Central Statistical Office: Household budget survey, 1973, Vol. I: Summary results (Dublin, Stationery Office, 1976).

2 idem: National income and expenditure, 1979 (Dublin, Stationery Office, 1981).

Appendix 9.1: Adjusted number of households by weekly household disposable income and household size (Ireland, 1973)

Household disposable income (pounds/week)	Household size				
	1-2	3-4	5-6	7+	Total
-20	1 655	347	111	50	2 163
20-40	712	1 147	716	390	2 965
40-70	212	655	611	480	1 958
70-	62	177	179	244	662
Total	2 641	2 326	1 615	1 164	7 748

Source: Central Statistical Office, Dublin.

10. KENYA

(J. Vandermoortele, ILO, Nairobi)

Summary

Kenya's income distribution estimate is based on a Social Accounting Matrix[1] which provides income estimates, adjusted to National Accounts and disaggregated according to socio-economic groups. The income concept used household available income. The inequality of income within socio-economic groups is estimated on the basis of proxies. For urban households, the Nairobi household survey was used; for smallholders, the distribution of household consumption and for other rural households the distribution of land. In the last two cases, a special relationship was used in order to make the transition between respectively the consumption and land distribution, and the income distribution. It is assumed that incomes between and within socio-economic groups are log-normally distributed so that the estimation of total income distribution can be estimated. Results are available on the distributions of available income per household and per head.

1. Introduction

The estimate of Kenya's income distribution, presented in this chapter, is based not directly on a national household survey but on a Social Accounting Matrix (SAM). The SAM or the extended input-output table is an alternative presentation of the National Accounts, which provides information not only on economic aggregates, such as income and consumption, but also on their distribution. In the case of Kenya, sub-aggregates were estimated for various socio-economic groups, thereby providing an estimate of between-group inequality. However, the estimation of the total inequality requires an estimate of the inequality within each group as well.

In order to relate the distribution of income within each group to the total income inequality, one needs to know something about the statistical property of the distribution function as a whole. There are good reasons to assume that the income distribution in each group follows a so-called "log-normal distribution".

Indeed, empirical research in other countries confirms that the log-normal distribution is in accordance with observed income data.[2] It gives a good fit in the middle-income brackets, covering more than 60 per cent of the population. One important property is that when the total distribution is log-normal, and when the individual components of that distribution are found to be log-normal, then the total distribution can be easily calculated on the basis of within-group inequalities.

An additional property of the log-normal distribution is its efficient estimation methods, following from its close relationship with the normal distribution.

2.   Estimation of inequality within
      socio-economic groups

The Kenyan Social Accounting Matrix uses the following household concept: a group of persons eating and living together and operating a common cash account.   Income is defined as total available income of private households.   It includes income in cash, as well as in kind, the market value of own-produced consumption, the imputed rent, the domestic transfers and the transfers with the rest of the world.

The Social Accounting Matrix further distinguishes the following eight socio-economic groups: the poor, middle-income and rich urban households, rural households in four different farm size classes: less than 0.5 ha, between 0.5 and 1.0 ha, between 1.0 and 8.0 ha, and more than 8.0 ha, as well as other rural households.   The number of households in each group had to be estimated on the basis of the 1969 and 1979 population censuses.[3] However, it is only possible to estimate accurately the number of households for the following three groups: (i) urban households;   (ii) rural smallholders;   and (iii) other rural households.   The income figures of the SAM have been aggregated accordingly.

The income distribution within the groups was estimated on the basis of the following surveys:

(i)   the Nairobi Household Budget Survey[4] for the urban household incomes;

(ii)   the distribution of household consumption among smallholders;[5] and

(iii)   the distribution of land[6] for the other rural households.

The first proxy was chosen because the Nairobi Household Budget Survey covered over 50 per cent of the total urban population.

The second proxy, the distribution of consumption among smallholders, is taken from the first Integrated Rural Survey, IRS 1 (1974), since IRS 2 (1976) did not collect data on income and consumption.   The income figures reported in IRS 1 show a large number of households with negative income, but with high levels of consumption.   This is because of a negative change in the livestock valuation between the start and the end of the survey.   It is clear that these reporting errors overestimate the true income inequality among smallholders. Therefore, Collier and Lal[7] adjusted the reported income figures (for Nyanza Province only). They exclude the transient changes in the valuation of livestock and replace it by the concept of a permanent livestock income which leaves the value of the herd unchanged. In doing so, their provincial income distribution was 30 per cent more equal than the original reported incomes in the province. However, the present approach towards the problem of poor income data of IRS 1 is different. Total household consumption is considered as the best proxy for permanent or long-term household income, because the level of consumption is relatively insensitive to income variability in the short run. Moreover, the collected consumption data are generally fairly accurate and reliable.

The last proxy (table 10.1), the distribution of land, appears to be very unequal. It is generally acknowledged that the concentration of land is higher than the concentration of income and consumption because farm size is normally negatively correlated with the intensity of land utilisation.

However, there is no consensus on the extent of disparity between the concentration ratios, since this is largely determined by country-specific institutions (e.g. the tenure system, the importance of the agricultural sector, the tax system, the wage policy, etc.).

In the case of Kenya, however, there is an indicator for the disparity between the concentration ratio of land and income. The land gini index, as derived from the IRS 1 data, equals 0.455, while the income concentration ratio (as proxied by consumption) is equal to 0.382. If one assumes that in the Kenyan context the discrepancy between both gini ratios has the same magnitude for "other rural" households as for smallholders, one can derive another estimate of the income inequality among the "other rural" households. The gini ratio of this proxy distribution is 16 per cent lower than that of the proxy distribution based upon land concentration. Hence the adjusted proxy distribution reflects more accurately the very high income inequality within the heterogeneous group of rural households.

3. Total income distribution

The total income distribution can now be estimated, if one can prove that the proxy distributions are log-normally distributed. It was found[8] that this is indeed the case, so that one can derive the total income distribution, using the decomposability property of the log-normal distribution.[9] The application of this property generates the following decile income distribution (table 10.2).

Table 10.1: The decile distribution of the proxy distributions (in percentages)

Decile	Urban households	Smallholders' consumption distribution	Land distribution
	(1)	(2)	(3)
I	1.3	2.2	0.0
II	2.4	3.5	0.7
III	3.1	4.8	1.0
IV	3.7	6.1	1.2
V	5.0	7.3	2.2
VI	6.1	8.6	2.6
VII	7.8	10.7	4.4
VIII	12.9	12.5	5.5
IX	16.9	15.6	9.7
X	40.7	28.6	73.0
Gini index	0.52	0.38	0.81

Sources: (1) Central Bureau of Statistics: Nairobi household budget survey, 1974 (Nairobi, unpublished).

(2) idem: Integrated rural survey, 1974 (own tabulation) (Nairobi).

(3) idem: Integrated rural survey, 1976 (Nairobi, unpublished); idem: A brief review of farming activities, 1976; idem: Gap-farm survey, 1979 (Nairobi, unpublished).

Table 10.2: Distribution of adjusted household available income (in percentages); per household and per head (Kenya, 1977)

Decile	Per household (%)	Per head
I	0.9	0.8
II	1.8	1.7
III	2.6	2.6
IV	3.7	3.6
V	4.9	4.8
VI	6.6	6.4
VII	8.9	8.7
VIII	10.3	10.1
IX	14.6	16.4
X	45.8	45.0
Gini index	0.59	0.59

These estimates are of the same magnitude as those found by Anker and Knowles.[10]

Notes

[1] Central Bureau of Statistics: Social Accounting Matrix - 1976: A revised edition (Nairobi, 1981).

[2] J. Aitchison and J. Brown: The log-normal distribution (Cambridge, Cambridge University Press, 1957); N.C. Kakwani: Income inequality and poverty (Oxford, Oxford University Press, 1980).

[3] Central Bureau of Statistics: Kenya population census, 1969 (Nairobi, 1970); idem: Kenya population census, 1979 (Nairobi, unpublished).

[4] idem: <u>Nairobi household budget survey, 1974</u> (Nairobi, unpublished).

[5] idem: <u>Integrated rural survey, 1974/75</u> (Nairobi, 1977).

[6] The land concentration ratio is obtained from a combination of the following data: idem: <u>Integrated rural survey II - 1976/77</u> (Nairobi, unpublished) for the land distribution among smallholders; idem: <u>Gap-farm survey, 1979</u> (Nairobi, unpublished) for the land distribution among gap farmers; and idem: <u>A brief review of farming activities, 1976</u> (Nairobi).

[7] P. Collier and D. Lal: <u>Poverty and growth in Kenya</u>, Working Paper No. 389 (washington DC, World Bank, 1980).

[8] J. Vandermoortele and R. van der Hoeven: <u>Income distribution and consumption patterns in urban and rural Kenya and by socio-economic groups</u> (Geneva, ILO, 1982; mimeographed World Employment Programme research working paper; restricted).

[9] ibid., p. 7.

[10] R. Anker and J.C. Knowles: <u>Population growth, employment and economic-demographic interactions in Kenya: Bachue - Kenya</u> (Aldershot, Hampshire, Gower Publishing; New York, St. Martin's Press, 1983), p. 442.

11. MEXICO (1968)

(W. van Ginneken, ILO, Geneva)

Summary

The Mexican income distribution estimates are based on the 1968 Household Survey. The income concept employed in this survey is household available income. Various income sources were adjusted to National Accounts totals. Three types of income distribution estimates were generated: household available income per household, per head and per equivalent unit.

1. Introduction

The income distribution estimates presented in this chapter are based on the 1968 Household Survey carried out by the Mexican Bank[1] and tabulated by the President's Secretariat.[2] For this study, we had the use of the computer tape[3] including the individual household data so that we were able to generate any desired tabulations. During the seventies two more household surveys were carried out: one by the National Labour Information and Statistics Centre[4] (1975) and one by the Programming and Budget Ministry (1977). The 1975 survey was less reliable than the 1968 survey,[5] when compared with National Accounts, while the results of the 1977 survey were not yet published at the time of writing. Altimir[6] already adjusted the 1968 survey data for inconsistencies with National Accounts, but this chapter will go further in a number of aspects. In particular, it will estimate the distribution of income per head and per equivalent unit.

For the 1968 survey, 5,608 households were interviewed during the last week of March 1968. The reference period for income was one year. The household definition used by the survey is all "persons living together in one house and who share - albeit partially - income, food and expenditure". This concept corresponds to the household definition employed for other countries. There was no need to adjust the household size distribution because the tape with the individual household information also included weighing factors so as to make them consistent with national population estimates.

2. Consistency with National Accounts

The 1968 survey reports available income, which includes wages and salaries, income from self-employment, income from capital and investments, and cash transfers. All income items exclude direct

taxes as well as employers' and employees' contributions to social
security.   They include, however, income in kind such as consumption
from own produce and imputed rent for owner-occupied houses.

Altimir[7] has already estimated the corresponding totals of
National Accounts, and for comparative purposes we add the aggregated
total as measured by the 1968 survey (table 11.1).   However, we
adjusted Altimir's data marginally[8] (by about 7.5 per cent) since
the reference period for the 1968 survey income data is between 1
April 1967 and 31 March 1968, and not between 1 January and
31 December 1968.

Table 11.1:   Aggregated available household income as measured by the
1968   survey   and   National   Accounts   data
(1 April 1967-31 March 1968) (in millions of pesos)

Sources of income	1968 survey	National Accounts	Ratio of 100* (1)/(2)
	(1)	(2)	(3)
Net wages and salaries	98 014	95 706	102.4
Entrepreneurial income	45 866	99 886	45.9
Income from capital	21 429*	44 516	48.1
Transfers	5 912	7 599	77.8
Total	171 221	247 707	69.1

* Including "other income".

Table 11.2:   Double-log   food   expenditure   functions   (household available   income   is   adjusted   for   National   Accounts), Mexico, 1968

							Economies-of-scale factor
Log F	= a	+ b log Y		+ c log N	R^2		(e)
	1.136	0.433		0.319	0.56		0.563
		(0.006)		(0.014)			
Log (F/N)	= a	+ b log (Y/N)		− t log N	R^2		e
	1.045	0.464		0.230	0.61		0.571
		(0.002)		(0.011)			

3.   Estimating equivalent scales

Table 11.2 shows the double-log food expenditure functions which served as a base for calculating the economies-of-scale factor.

The subsequent calculations used the value of 0.563 for the economies-of-scale factor, since the first equation in table 11.2 is probably less affected by multi-collinearity.

Table 11.3 shows that the adjustment has fairly little impact on measured inequality. Even though about one-third of national available income is not accounted for in the household survey (see table 11.1), the gini index increases only by about four percentage points. This is probably due to the fact that underestimated income from self-employment is fairly equally distributed over all income classes. The adjustment for capital income, which accrues exclusively to the highest household quintile, does increase the highest decile by about three to four percentage points, since the proportion of capital income in that decile is particularly high.

Table 11.3: Distribution of household available income (in percentages); original data and data adjusted for National Accounts; per household, per capita and per equivalent unit (Mexico, 1968)

Type of adjustment	Original data			Adjusted for National Accounts		
Income concept[1]	I	II	III	I	II	III
Recipient unit	House-hold (1)	Person (2)	Person (3)	House-hold (4)	Person (5)	Person (6)
Deciles						
I	1.0	1.0	1.0	0.7	0.7	0.7
II	2.2	2.1	2.3	2.0	1.9	2.0
III	3.0	3.0	3.1	2.8	2.6	2.8
IV	4.1	3.9	4.1	3.6	3.5	3.6
V	5.1	4.9	5.1	4.5	4.4	4.5
VI	6.4	6.2	6.5	5.7	5.7	5.8
VII	8.3	8.0	8.3	7.5	7.4	7.8
VIII	11.2	10.7	11.1	10.6	9.9	10.3
IX	16.4	16.1	16.1	15.9	15.5	15.6
X	42.3	44.2	42.2	46.7	48.5	46.9
Gini-index	0.53	0.54	0.52	0.56	0.58	0.56

[1] I: available household income;
II: available household income per head;
III: available household income per equivalent unit.

Note: Deciles are computed on the basis of individual household observations; gini index is based on deciles.

An unexpected result of table 11.3 is that the distribution of persons by income per head is more unequal than the distribution of households by household income. One would have expected the opposite since the concept of household income per head seems to imply a certain averaging of income variation.[9] The reason is that the economies-of-scale factor for Mexico is much lower than in other countries.

Notes

[1] Banco de México: La distribución del ingreso en México 1974: Encuesta sobre los ingresos y gastos de las familias (Mexico, DF, Fondo de Cultura Ecónomica, 1974).

[2] Dirección General Coordinadora de la Programación Económica y Social: Estudios de ingresos y gastos de las familias (Mexico, DF, Secretaría de la Presidencia, 1974; mimeographed).

[3] I thank Dr. Solís and Dr. Vera for their help in this matter.

[4] Centro Nacional de Información y Estadísticas de Trabajo: Encuesta de ingresos y gastos familiares, 1975 (Mexico, DF, 1977).

[5] W. van Ginneken: Socio-economic groups and income distribution in Mexico (London, Croom Helm, 1980). Some analyses on this survey have been published: see, for example, G. Vera Ferrer: El tamaño de la familia y la distribución del ingreso en México: Un ensayo exploratorio (Banco de México, Subdirección de Investigación Económica, Dec. 1980).

[6] O. Altimir: Las estimaciones de la distribución del ingreso en México (Santiago de Chile, CEPAL, 1979; mimeographed).

[7] ibid.

[8] We took 75 per cent of total disposable income in 1967 and 25 per cent of that in 1968.

[9] We do not know of any work which has demonstrated under what conditions the gini index of household income inequality is higher than that of household income per head.

12. NEPAL (1976-77)

(S. Kansal, World Bank, Washington, DC)

Summary

The income distribution estimates for Nepal are based on the 1976-77 Survey of Employment, Income Distribution and Consumption Patterns. The income concept used for the estimate is gross available income, i.e. before tax. Some adjustments were made to correct for inconsistency with National Accounts. First, rural landless households whose heads did not report an occupation were included, and secondly, imputed rental income and the value of freely collected fuel wood were distributed across income classes. The study estimates the distributions of gross available income per household in both rural and urban areas.

1. Data source

The basic data source for deriving household income distribution in Nepal is the 1976-77 Survey of Employment, Income Distribution and Consumption Patterns in Nepal, conducted by the National Planning Commission.

Prior to that, in 1973-75, the Nepal Rashtra Bank (the Central Bank of Nepal) had conducted a household budget survey in the urban areas; data were collected on household income, expenditures and living conditions. However, the reported income figures obtained from the 1973-75 survey were not sufficiently reliable for the classification of households by income levels, and in the reports from the 1973-75 survey, total consumption expenditures were used to derive income distribution data.

2. Brief description of the 1976-77 survey

The 1976-77 survey covered all private households, excluding institutional ones. The sample covered 4,040 rural households (about 0.19 per cent of total rural households) and 940 urban households (about 0.82 per cent of total urban households). The survey was conducted during March-July 1977, with a reference period in rural areas of 16 July 1976 to 15 July 1977 and in urban areas of 16 April 1976 to 15 April 1977. The data were collected through the interview method.

For income data, a household was defined as a group of persons related by blood, marriage or adoption that generally shared a common kitchen. A single person was treated as a household if he/she maintained a kitchen.

Household income was defined as the aggregate income (before deduction of taxes) of all household members. It included both income in cash and in kind and transfer receipts, but excluded the imputed value of owner-occupied and free dwellings and the collection of free materials (mainly fuelwood) used in domestic consumption.

3. Evaluation of the 1976-77 survey

The rate of non-enumeration (including non-response) was negligible as data were collected from 4,969 sample households (4,037 rural and 932 urban), almost identical in size to the planned sample of 4,980 households (4,040 rural and 940 urban). However, in the survey report, rural income distribution was based on information from only 3,664 households (giving a 9.2 per cent non-utilisation rate), apparently because those households where the head of household reported no occupation (373) were omitted. It seems that these 373 households were left out erroneously.

The survey definition of household income excluded the value of imputed rentals from owner-occupied and free houses and the collection of free domestic materials. National Accounts statistics showed that the imputed rental income from owner-occupied and free houses and the imputed value of free fuelwood was about Rs.1,600 million in 1976-77, accounting for about 9.3 per cent of total gross domestic product in Nepal.

The survey estimate of total household income (Rs.13,517 million) was lower by about 13 per cent than that derived from the National Accounts and budget data (Rs.15,500 million). This difference seems to be mainly the result of the exclusion of imputed incomes from the survey data. When adjusted, the estimate of total household income worked out to be Rs.15,125 million, very close to the National Accounts-based estimate of Rs.15,500 million.

4. Derivation of income distribution

The adjusted household income distribution estimates were derived by making four adjustments to the original survey data.

First, the 373 rural households where the head of the household did not report an occupation were included in the rural income distribution. They were assumed to belong to the "landless households" category. Based on their average income, they were distributed between the two appropriate income classes such that the overall average income of these households was equal to that of the landless households included in the survey.

Second, the imputed rental income (Rs.929 million) was distributed across the different income classes. This was done by using the survey estimates of the average number of rooms occupied by the households in the different income classes.

Third, the imputed value of free fuelwood collected by family members (Rs.680 million or Rs.298 per household) was distributed among the different income classes. Rs.298 was added to each income class, based on the assumption that the collection of free fuel is more prevalent in the lower-income classes, but at the same time the total expenditure on fuel and light (imputed plus actual) of upper-income households is much higher than that of lower-income households.

Finally, the adjusted income distribution for the country was derived by combining the rural and urban household income distributions using the total number of households in the two areas as weights.

Table 12.1 shows the adjusted income distribution by deciles of households and the gini index.

5. Concluding remarks

The household income distribution in Nepal was derived from the country's first nation-wide household survey. The results show that rural income inequality is slightly greater than its urban counterpart. This may be the result, in part, of the highly unequal distribution of agricultural land holdings and, in part, because of the nature of the classification of the urban-rural areas. Some of the village panchayats that are included in rural areas have more people than some of the town panchayats (included in urban areas). Thus, the so-called rural sector seems to include some areas which are basically urban. Therefore, observed rural income inequality should not really be viewed as an indicator of rural inequality.

Table 12.1: Distribution of adjusted gross household available income (in percentages), Nepal, 1976-77

Deciles (households)	Rural	Urban	Total
I	1.8	1.9	1.8
II	2.8	2.9	2.8
III	3.4	3.7	3.4
IV	4.7	4.4	4.6
V	5.3	5.9	5.2
VI	6.5	6.2	6.5
VII	7.3	7.4	7.5
VIII	9.2	10.4	9.0
IX	12.4	14.6	12.7
X	46.6	42.6	46.5
Gini index	0.53	0.49	0.53

Appendix 12.1: Distribution of households, average income per household, and share of income by income classes, urban Nepal, 1976-77

Annual income classes (Rs.)	Sample households		Annual average household income (Rs.)	Share of income	
	Nos.	%		%	Cum. %
(1)	(2)	(3)	(4)	(5)	(6)
1. below 500	3	0.32	333[1]	0.01	0.01
2. 500- 1 500	28	3.00	1 000	0.28	0.29
3. 1 500- 2 500	95	10.19	2 000	1.87	2.16
4. 2 500- 3 500	92	9.87	3 000	2.72	4.88
5. 3 500- 4 000	67	7.19	3 750	2.48	7.36
6. 4 000- 5 000	106	11.37	4 500	4.71	12.07
7. 5 000- 8 000	212	22.75	6 500	13.60	25.67
8. 8 000-10 000	80	8.58	9 000	7.10	32.77
9. 10 000-15 000	111	11.91	12 500	13.69	46.46
10. 15 000-25 000	75	8.05	20 000	14.80	61.26
11. 25 000-40 000	31	3.33	32 500	9.93	71.19
12. 40 000-75 000	16	1.72	57 500	9.08	80.27
13. 75 000 and above	16	1.72	125 000	19.73	100.00
14. All classes	932	100.00		100.00	

[1] Average household income is taken to be two-thirds of the upper limit of the income class following Mehran's Portable Method. See F. Mehran: Dealing with grouped income distribution data (Geneva, ILO, 1975; mimeographed World Employment Programme research working paper; restricted).

Source: National Planning Commission: A survey of employment, income distribution and consumption patterns in Nepal, 1976-77.

Appendix 12.2: Distribution of households, average income per household, and share of income by income classes, rural Nepal, 1976-77

Annual income classes (Rs.)	Sample households		Annual average household income (Rs.)	Share of income	
	Nos.	%		%	Cum. %
(1)	(2)	(3)	(4)	(5)	(6)
1. below 500	132	3.60	333[1]	0.16	0.16
2. 500- 1 500	441	12.04	1 000	1.63	1.79
3. 1 500- 2 500	634	17.30	2 000	4.70	6.49
4. 2 500- 3 500	597	16.30	3 000	6.64	13.13
5. 3 500- 4 000	265	7.23	3 750	3.68	16.81
6. 4 000- 5 000	359	9.80	4 500 .	5.99	22.80
7. 5 000- 8 000	553	15.09	6 500	13.32	36.12
8. 8 000-10 000	189	5.16	9 000	6.31	42.43
9. 10 000-15 000	180	4.91	12 500	8.34	50.77
10. 15 000-25 000	115	3.14	20 000	8.53	59.30
11. 25 000-40 000	89	2.43	32 500	10.72	70.02
12. 40 000-75 000	78	2.13	57 500	16.63	86.65
13. 75 000 and above	32	0.87	112 500	13.35	100.00
14. All classes	3 664	100.00		100.00	

[1] Average household income is taken to be two-thirds of the upper limit of the income class, following Mehran's Portable method.   See F. Mehran: Dealing with grouped income distribution data (Geneva, ILO, 1975; mimeographed World Employment Programme research working paper; restricted).

Source: National Planning Commission: A survey of employment, income distribution and consumption patterns in Nepal, 1976-77.

13. <u>PANAMA</u> (1976)

(J.-G. Park, World Bank, Washington, DC)

Summary

The Panamanian income distribution estimates are based on the 1976 Special Survey on Household Income. The income concept used in this survey is gross available household income (i.e. before tax). Aggregated gross available household income - as measured by the survey - was only 5 per cent lower than the corresponding National Accounts total. Two groups who were not included in the survey were included in the estimates: a small group of farm households belonging to the lowest quintile of the income distribution and some employers and self-employed in the metropolitan areas. The study generated the distribution of gross available income per household for the metropolitan area, the rest of the country and the country as a whole.

1. Data source

The 1970 Encuesta Especial sobre Ingresos a través de los Hogares (EEIH or Special Survey on Household Income) was the first nation-wide sample survey on household income in Panama. It was carried out by the Dirección de Estadística y Censo, with technical assistance from the United Nations Development Programme.

2. Brief description of 1970 survey

The survey covered all private households in the country, except those located in the Panama Canal Zone (mostly foreign households) and in areas where access was difficult. The survey sample contained 5,185 private households (about 2.0 per cent of total households in the country). Out of the total sample, 2,374 households were from metropolitan areas and 2,811 from the rest of the country.

The survey was conducted during January and March 1971 through interviews. The reference period was the calendar year 1970.

A household was defined as a single person or group of persons living together under family conditions. It included boarders, relatives, guests and domestic workers living permanently in the household. It also included persons who normally were members of the household but were absent during a part of the reference period for work, study, medical care or vacation. Household income was defined as before-tax income and included income, both in cash and in kind (including imputed income) and transfers.

Table 13.1: Distribution of adjusted gross available household income
(in percentages), Panama, 1970

Deciles (households)	Metropolitan areas	Rest of the country	Total country
I	0.9	1.0	0.7
II	2.0	1.8	1.3
III	3.3	2.5	2.0
IV	4.3	3.2	3.2
V	5.4	4.2	4.7
VI	6.8	6.2	6.3
VII	8.9	8.8	8.4
VIII	11.8	12.0	11.6
IX	16.3	17.9	17.6
X	40.3	42.4	44.2
Gini index	0.51	0.55	0.57

3. Evaluation of the 1970 survey

Information on household income was collected from 4,460
households out of the total sample of 5,185, giving a relatively high
non-enumeration rate of 14 per cent.[1]

The EEIH survey report gave information on the composition of the
labour force in terms of employees and non-employees. A comparison
with the results of labour force surveys conducted separately suggest
that the EEIH survey under-represented non-employees (employers and
self-employed), particularly those in non-agricultural activities in
metropolitan areas, which might have introduced a bias towards a more
equal distribution of income. The survey also under-represented
employees in the agricultural sector but over-represented them in the
non-agricultural sector. For the country as a whole, however, the
coverage of employees was almost complete.

The survey estimate of total household income amounted to 678.5 million balboas. This was 95 per cent of the comparable aggregate income of 713.8 million balboas derived from the National Accounts.

The average income of employee households was significantly higher than that of non-employee households. This was true in both the metropolitan and the non-metropolitan areas and in both the agricultural and the non-agricultural sectors. The relatively higher average income of employee households in comparison with non-employee households in the agricultural sector may largely be explained by the fact that over 40 per cent of all farm families in Panama are subsistence farmers. On the other hand, workers on commercial farms (e.g. banana plantations) account for about half of all agricultural wage workers and receive relatively high wages. The relatively lower average income of non-employee households in comparison with employee households in the metropolitan, non-agricultural sector appears to be unrealistic. The survey probably left out some income-earning household members in the non-employee households in the non-agricultural sectors.

4.   Derivation of income distribution

The under-reporting of overall income in the 1970 EEIH survey was not sizeable. However, the survey's under-coverage of the non-employee households suggests that the survey data may have some systematic bias in the distribution of household income.

Data on the composition of the labour force suggests that the non-employee households in the rest of the country which were not covered by the survey were mainly farm households. Survey data on income distribution in the rest of the country also show that the two lowest income classes have a relatively low ratio of income earners to total household members. It was therefore assumed that non-employee income earners in the non-metropolitan areas who were left out from the survey belonged to the two lowest income classes. Thus, the adjusted distribution of household income for the rest of the country was derived after adjusting the total income of the lowest income classes for the exclusion of the non-employee income earners.

With respect to the non-employee income earners in the metropolitan areas who were not covered in the survey, it was assumed that their income distribution patterns were the same as those of the non-employee income earners who were covered in the survey. Thus, the survey data on the distribution of income of non-employees in metropolitan areas were adjusted upward, so that the sum of the adjusted incomes in metropolitan areas and the rest of the country was equal to the total personal income in the National Accounts.

Table 13.1 gives the adjusted income distribution by deciles of households for metropolitan areas, for the rest of the country and for the country as a whole.

5.   Concluding remarks

The income inequality in the household income distribution in Panama is relatively high.   This may reflect the dualistic structure of the country's economy (i.e. the coexistence of a large number of subsistence farms and well-developed commercial farms and modern services).   However, income in the survey referred to gross household income before payment of direct taxes.   To the extent that the rate of taxation is progressive, the income distribution estimates derived from the survey data may overstate income inequality.

The survey data used for this analysis appear to be of good quality in general.   However, the data on the income of non-employee households may be less reliable because of the long recall period used in the survey.   Non-employee households probably had difficulty in recalling their incomes, which often was irregular.

Note

1 Non-enumeration includes non-response.   Other reasons for non-enumeration could be either a vacant house or the inability of the enumerator to contact the sample household.

Appendix 13.1: Distribution of total household income (unadjusted), Panama, 1970.

Average household income (balboas)	Household size	Number of households ('000)	Household factor income ('000 balboas)	Total household income ('000 balboas)
144	3.97	28.5	3 848	4 131
300	4.91	28.5	7 772	8 538
513	4.67	28.5	13 287	14 611
831	4.73	28.5	20 519	23 690
1 216	4.91	28.5	32 102	34 669
1 645	4.91	28.5	43 299	46 874
2 183	4.86	28.5	58 218	62 205
3 008	5.20	28.5	79 891	85 739
4 521	5.34	28.5	118 537	128 860
11 056	5.41	28.5	300 993	315 085
Total	4.89	285.3	678 466	724 402

Source: Dirección de Estadística y Censo: Encuesta Especial sobre Ingresos a través de los Hogares; Año 1970: Estadística Panameña, Año XXXIV, Suplemento, 1975, pp. 66-67

14. PHILIPPINES (1970-71)

(B. Rao, World Bank, Jakarta)

Summary

The Philippines income distribution estimates are based on the 1970-71 Family Income and Expenditure Survey. The income concept used in the survey is gross family available income (i.e. before tax). For families whose recorded expenditures exceeded recorded income, expenditures were taken as a proxy for income. For the higher income classes savings were estimated and added respectively to incomes in urban areas and to expenditures in rural areas. After these adjustments, total gross available income was 6 per cent lower than the corresponding National Accounts total. The study generated the distributions of gross available income per household for urban and rural areas and for the country as a whole.

1. Data sources

The Family Income and Expenditure Surveys (FIES), which have been conducted at approximately five-year intervals since 1956, are the principal sources for estimating income distribution in the Philippines. The most recent survey at the time of writing refers to 1975, but the data have not been fully tabulated or analysed.[1] Thus, the 1971 FIES data were used for deriving a distribution of household income in the country.

2. Brief description of the 1971 survey

The survey was conducted in May 1971 by the National Census and Statistical Office, with May 1970 to April 1971 as the reference period. The survey sample included 11,659 households, about 0.2 per cent of the total households in the country. The data were collected through interviews.

Although the household was the ultimate sampling unit, income and expenditure data were collected for families. The household was defined as a group of persons living together in the same dwelling and eating together in the same kitchen. The family was defined as the members of a household related to the head by blood, marriage or adoption. A person living alone was considered as a separate family. Household income was defined as the aggregate of the before-tax income of family members only. It included income in cash and in kind, transfers and imputed rents from owner-occupied dwellings.

The survey report also provided annual data on family
expenditures. Expenditures on food, beverages and tobacco were
collected for the week preceding the date of interview; for several
other regularly consumed items, average weekly or monthly expenditures
were the basis for annual figures. For durable goods, actual
expenditures during the previous 12-month period were obtained.
Personal taxes were included in expenditures.

3. Evaluation of the 1971 survey

Since the 1971 survey used the 1970 census as the sampling frame,
there was no significant discrepancy in terms of the coverage and
representativeness of the sample. For instance, the population
estimate obtained from the survey (36.5 million) was very close to the
census count of 37.8 million on 1 May 1970.

A comparison of the survey estimate of total family income with
those based on the National Accounts data showed that the former were
about 68 per cent of the latter, an under-reporting of about 32 per
cent. On the other hand, the under-reporting of consumption
expenditures was only 6 per cent, suggesting that the survey has
covered consumption expenditures quite adequately.

The survey results were tabulated to show average family income
and expenditures by different income levels. They indicated that as
many as 94 per cent of the families spent more than they earned. For
the entire country, the survey showed negative personal savings (minus
4,700 million pesos), as against positive savings of about
4,000 million pesos derived from the National Accounts statistics.
This finding confirms that income was significantly under-reported in
the survey, even though some families in the lower income groups may
have experienced dissavings.

4. Derivation of income distribution

In addition to data on average household income and expenditures
by income class, the 1971 survey yielded data on the distribution of
expenditures by expenditure class. The adjusted income distribution
estimates given here were derived using the latter data.

The survey data showed that, in rural areas, expenditures for the
first ten income classes (with an average income of up to 5,500 pesos)
were consistently higher than income. As noted earlier, the survey
under-reported incomes, and expenditures were therefore assumed to
represent actual incomes for these ten income classes. Thus, for
expenditures up to 5,500 pesos, the distribution of expenditures by
expenditure classes was taken as a proxy for income distribution.
For the higher expenditure classes (with average expenditures above
5,500 pesos), average household savings were estimated from the survey

results by using an aggregate relationship between family income and expenditures for these high-income households. The rural distribution of income for the higher expenditure classes was obtained by combining the distributions of expenditures and of savings.

A similar procedure was followed for urban areas, except that average expenditures up to 7,000 pesos were considered to be the proxy for income, instead of cutting off at 5,500 pesos as for the rural areas. Income distribution by deciles of families and the gini index are given in table 14.1.

Table 14.1: Distribution of adjusted gross family available income (in percentages), Philippines, 1970-71

Deciles (families)	Rural areas	Urban areas	Total country
I	2.3	1.8	1.9
II	4.0	3.1	3.2
III	5.0	3.9	4.1
IV	5.9	4.7	4.9
V	6.8	5.6	5.8
VI	7.8	6.7	7.0
VII	9.8	8.3	8.5
VIII	11.3	11.6	10.5
IX	14.8	17.8	15.3
X	32.1	36.4	38.8
Gini index	0.39	0.47	0.46

5.   Concluding remarks

Average family income as derived from the adjusted income distribution was 5,157 pesos, about 94 per cent of the average income derived from the National Accounts (5,481 pesos).   Total family savings amounted to 3,900 million pesos, close to the 4,000 million pesos estimated on the basis of the National Accounts. The pattern of family income distribution for the country as a whole generally followed that of urban areas, revealing more inequality than in rural areas.

Note

[1] The World Bank's regional office had access to unpublished preliminary data, supplied on a confidential basis.   Its review suggests that under-reporting of household income was much more severe in the 1975 survey than in the 1971 survey.   It is generally agreed that the 1975 survey did not cover the upper income groups adequately and that the 1971 survey appears to have had better coverage.

Appendix 14.1: Gross family income distribution in the Philippines, 1970-71 (published data)

Income class (pesos/year)	Urban areas			Rural areas			Total country		
	Number of families	Average family income	Average family expenditure	Number of families	Average family income	Average family expenditure	Number of families	Average family income	Average family expenditure
	('000)	(pesos)	(pesos)	('000)	(pesos)	(pesos)	('000)	(pesos)	(pesos)
Less than 500	37	305	1 913	292	341	1 607	329	337	1 641
500- 1 000	67	741	2 253	700	755	1 985	767	754	2 009
1 000- 1 500	107	1 258	2 774	666	1 248	2 407	773	1 250	2 458
1 500- 2 000	133	1 766	3 546	615	1 738	2 822	748	1 743	2 951
2 000- 2 500	164	2 272	3 743	447	2 236	3 225	611	2 245	3 364
2 500- 3 000	166	2 750	4 114	351	2 741	3 601	517	2 744	3 766
3 000- 4 000	290	3 453	4 972	505	3 442	3 926	795	3 446	4 307
4 000- 5 000	187	4 462	5 858	288	4 446	4 744	475	4 452	5 182
5 000- 6 000	148	5 442	6 833	168	5 467	5 482	316	5 455	6 114
6 000- 8 000	211	6 871	8 208	192	6 861	6 505	403	6 866	7 397
8 000-10 000	135	8 913	9 799	91	8 903	8 082	226	8 909	9 107
10 000-15 000	161	12 086	12 733	74	11 792	9 115	235	11 994	11 594
15 000-20 000	52	17 222	17 014	19	16 740	12 643	71	17 092	15 832
20 000+	55	33 441	21 990	26	28 239	12 551	81	31 746	18 915
All classes	1 913	5 867	6 810	4 434	2 818	3 474	6 347	3 736	4 479

Source: Family income and expenditure survey, 1971.

15. SIERRA LEONE (1967-69)

(S. Kamsal, World Bank, Washington, DC)

Summary

The income distribution estimates for Sierra Leone are based on the 1967-69 Household Budget Survey. Although the survey only measures monetary income, adjustments on the basis of expenditure data are made in order to arrive at gross available income (i.e. before tax). The study estimated the distributions of gross available income per household for urban and rural areas and for the country as a whole.

1. Data sources

The basic data source for estimating the income distribution statistics for Sierra Leone is the 1967-69 Household Budget Survey conducted by the country's Central Statistical Office. The other source is the 1974-75 household budget survey, conducted by the Department of Agricultural Economics, Michigan State University, in collaboration with the University of Sierra Leone. The 1974-75 survey was basically a rural household survey. However, it also collected data on urban household income as part of a study of rural-urban migration carried out in conjunction with the 1974-75 household survey.

2. A brief description of the 1967-69 survey

The 1967-69 survey covered all households in the country. It was conducted during 1967-68 in urban areas and during 1969 in rural areas. For household income and expenditures, the previous month was used as the reference period. For certain items the data were collected for the past one year.

The survey sample contained 3,331 households, constituting about 0.7 per cent of total households in the country. Out of the total sample, 1,193 households were from urban and 2,138 from rural areas.

A household was defined as a single person or group of persons living together who pool their resources to provide for food, clothing, housing and other living essentials. The survey report did not explicitly give the definition of household income. For income distribution purposes, household income covered only monetary incomes. It excluded all non-monetary incomes received in kind, home-produce consumption and the imputed rents of non-renter households.

3. Evaluation of the 1967-69
   survey and data adjustments

Although the survey sample included 1,193 urban and 2,138 rural households, the tabulated results were based on 912 urban and 1,768 rural households. This gave non-enumeration rates of 23 and 17 per cent respectively in the two areas. We assumed that the distribution of enumerated sample households in each area was representative of that area.

In the survey about 10 per cent of urban and 9 per cent of rural households had reported zero income. Many of these households owned consumer durable goods like refrigerators, fans, sewing machines, etc. We distributed these households in the four lowest income groups as their percentage owning durables were of the same order as those of these four income groups.

The survey report gave only the distribution of households by monetary income classes and did not provide the corresponding distribution of household incomes. We estimated average incomes by using Mehran's Portable Method, which assumes Pareto distribution in each income interval. The average incomes ·so derived were only for monetary incomes and excluded all non-monetary incomes. The important exclusions were the consumption of own-produce and the imputed rents of households owning their own house. We estimated average household non-monetary incomes by utilising the survey data on the distribution of household expenditures by income classes and added them to the monetary incomes in different income groups.

4. Derivation of household income
   distribution

The estimates of household income distribution as derived from the adjusted data are given in table 15.1, while the original income distribution estimates (including only monetary income) are shown in the appendix.

Table 15.1: Distribution of adjusted gross household income (in percentages), Sierra Leone, 1967-69

Deciles (households)	Rural areas	Urban areas	Total country
I	1.8	2.5	2.0
II	3.3	3.5	3.6
III	4.3	4.5	4.5
IV	5.2	5.3	5.1
V	6.2	6.0	5.8
VI	6.9	6.7	6.9
VII	8.9	8.6	8.8
VIII	10.9	11.0	10.8
IX	15.2	14.6	14.7
X	37.2	37.3	37.8
Gini index	0.45	0.44	0.44

The income inequalities implicit in the adjusted and original survey data are as follows:

	Household inequality (gini index)	
	Adjusted	Original
Urban	0.45	0.52
Rural	0.44	0.60
Combined	0.44	0.59

The rural income inequality, based on the original survey data, was unrealistically high as it covered only monetary income. With adjustments for inclusion of non-monetary incomes and under-reported incomes, it was reduced from 0.60 to 0.44. In urban areas too, the income inequality was considerably reduced from 0.52 to 0.45.

The data base of Sierra Leone's income distribution is relatively weak. Nevertheless, the adjusted income distribution data showed that the level of income inequality in Sierra Leone is of the same order as the inequality in other African countries.

In 1976 the Central Statistical Office conducted a comprehensive household survey. When the survey results become available, it is hoped that more reliable income distribution estimates will be available for a relatively recent period.

Appendix 15.1: Cumulative distribution of households and income by monthly monetary income groups, Sierra Leone, 1967-69[1]

Monthly monetary income	Urban		Rural		Urban and Rural	
	Households	Income	Households	Income	Households	Income
No income reported	10.5	-	8.8	-	9.2	-
Less than 10 Leones	16.8	0.7	37.6	5.0	33.2	3.8
Less than 20 Leones	31.5	5.7	60.6	17.1	54.4	13.8
Less than 30 Leones	52.3	17.5	72.6	27.6	68.3	24.7
Less than 40 Leones	66.8	29.1	80.9	37.8	77.9	35.3
Less than 60 Leones	80.9	45.2	90.3	54.3	88.3	51.7
Less than 80 Leones	87.9	56.4	94.2	63.9	92.9	61.8
Less than 100 Leones	91.7	64.2	95.5	68.0	94.7	66.9
Less than 200 Leones	97.8	85.0	98.4	83.2	98.3	83.9
All incomes	100.0	100.0	100.0	100.0	100.0	100.0
Gini index		0.52		0.60		0.59

1 Compiled from household budget surveys, 1967-69.

Source: Central Statistics Office: National Accounts of Sierra Leone, 1972-73 to 1976-77 (Freetown, June 1978), p. 47.

16. SPAIN (1973-74)

(W. van Ginneken, ILO, Geneva)

Summary

The Spanish income distribution estimates are based on the 1973-74 Family Budget Survey.[1] The income concept used in the survey is household available income. For each source of income, the survey results were adjusted to the corresponding National Accounts totals. The study generated the distributions of available income per household and per head.

1. Introduction

The data shown in this chapter are based on the household survey carried out by the National Institute of Statistics between July 1973 and June 1974. The population covered by the survey included all private households in the national territory at that time, that is, all rural and non-rural private households in 47 peninsular, three insular and two African provinces of Spain. The net sample size was 24,151 dwellings, with a corresponding 92,515 inhabitants. The basic sampling unit was the private household, defined as the individual or group of persons inhabiting the same dwelling or part of it and running a joint expenditure budget.

A two-stage stratified sampling design was used in the survey. In the first stage the census tracts were sampled and in the second stage the dwellings within the census tract were selected. Census tracts were defined as geographical areas with fewer than 2,500 inhabitants. No explicit definition of stratum was given in the survey. Two criteria were followed for the assignation of a census tract to a stratum: the relative demographic importance of the main administrative units (province and municipality), and the socio-economic status of the majority of (heads of) households belonging to the census tract.

The households were interviewed for one week during the period between July 1973 and June 1974. Since the reference period for questions on income is one year, the responses relate to the period between July 1972 and June 1974. The responses are, however, concentrated in the year 1973 and it is for that reason that the aggregated survey data are compared with the corresponding National Accounts data of 1973 (see section 3).

2. Consistency with population data

The data supplied by the National Institute of Statistics are five tables which cross-classify households according to eight income classes and five income sources (net income from labour, from self-employment, from capital, regular transfers and irregular income). One table is available for each household size (1, 2, 3, 4, 5+). Unfortunately, no tables were provided on the number of households or persons in each cell; only the marginal totals were available. As a result, we had to estimate the number of households and of persons in each cell by solving eight systems of five simultaneous equations. (In each cell average incomes for each of the five income sources are known for five household size classes.)

It was also necesary to check whether the distribution of households by household size as measured by the survey corresponds with that found for the population as a whole. The most recently available data for such a comparison comes from the 1970 census; this employs the family concept, which is somewhat more limited than the household concept used by the survey. The difference between both distributions is small and may be even due to the tendency towards smaller households which is noticeable in all developed countries. There is therefore no need to adjust the household size distribution as measured by the 1973-74 survey.

Finally, in order to estimate aggregated household income, as measured by the survey, we need to estimate the number of households on 31 December 1973. Assuming that average household size remained constant between 1970 and 1975, we estimated the number of households at 9,163,538[2] on 31 December 1973.

3. Consistency with National Accounts

The 1973-74 survey collects information on four income sources: net wages and salaries, net income from self-employment, net property income and transfer income. The sum of these four sources adds up to disposable household income because direct taxes are already deducted from each income source. Disposable income - as defined by the 1973-74 survey - is in fact the same as household available income, because income from own produce and imputed rent from owner-occupied housing are included in respectively net income from self-employment and net income from property. Contributions to and transfers from private insurance companies are, however, not included.

It is not possible to find data on direct taxes by income source, because direct taxes are normally perceived over total income. It is therefore necessary to distribute the total amount of direct taxes over three income sources. (It is assumed that no direct taxes are perceived on transfers.) We shall assume that direct taxes are paid in proportion of income. It is assumed that the National Accounts figures[3] do not distinguish between families and private institutions. Since we expect the importance of private institutions to be small, we shall not try to estimate their income. As a result, the National Accounts totals which are shown in table 16.1 overestimate household disposable income to some extent. In addition, there is a problem in matching the data on social transfers in the survey and National Accounts. In estimating the National Accounts total, all medical benefits were deducted because they are either directly paid to medical institutions or reimbursements for medical expenses. In addition, we have not included "private international transfers" and "various current transfers" since they may not be regularly received. Finally, it is not possible to find separate data on net income from self-employment and net income from property. As a simplifying hypothesis we assume that the degree of underestimation is the same for both sources of income. This assumption is normally found to be true for other countries.

Table 16.1: Aggregated household income as calculated from the 1973-74 survey and the corresponding National Accounts totals (in millions of pesetas)

	Survey (1973-74)	National Accounts (1973)	100* (1):(2)
	(1)	(2)	(3)
Net wages and salaries	1 200 286	1 705 086	70.4
Net income from self-employment	453 879	(787 867)	57.6
Net income from property	177 599	(308 476)	57.6
Regular transfers	182 199	244 133*	74.6
Household available income	2 013 963	3 045 562	66.1

* Medical benefits - which are deducted - were assumed to represent the same proportion of total transfers as in 1975 (data supplied to the ILO).

Table 16.2: Distribution of available household income (in percentages); per household and per head, adjusted and unadjusted for National Accounts (Spain, 1973-74)

Type of data	Original		Adjusted	
Income concept	I	II	I	II
Recipient unit	Household*	Person	Household*	Person
Deciles				
I	2.1	2.7	1.9	2.6
II	4.1	4.8	3.8	4.6
III	5.4	5.8	5.1	5.5
IV	6.8	6.4	6.5	6.2
V	7.2	8.3	6.9	7.6
VI	9.4	8.8	8.9	9.1
VII	10.7	10.0	10.2	10.5
VIII	12.9	12.4	12.7	12.2
IX	15.3	15.0	16.0	15.4
X	26.1	25.8	28.0	26.4
Gini index	0.35	0.32	0.37	0.34

* The eighth and ninth deciles have been adjusted by hand, since the decile percentages were close to each other.

I: household available income;
II: household available income per head.

4. Results

The estimates shown in this section are based on tables which were specially made for this project.[4] The tables show average incomes (of five income sources), cross-classified by eight income classes and five household size classes (1, 2, 3, 4, 5+). One problem is that the household size classification stops at five persons and more. As a result, this last class includes a large percentage of all households (i.e. 30.5 per cent) and an even larger percentage of persons (i.e. about 50 per cent). Making some simplifying assumptions, we tried to separately estimate average income for household size classes 5, 6 and 7+. The resulting decile distributions and gini indices were, however, hardly different from the estimates shown in table 16.2.

As in most other industrialised countries, inequality of the per household distribution is higher than the per head distribution. It can further be observed that adjustment for National Accounts has a fairly small impact on the distribution, in spite of the fact that aggregate household available income, as measured by the survey, underestimates the corresponding National Accounts total by about one-third.

Notes

[1] Ministerio de Planificación del Desarrollo, Instituto Nacional de Estadística: Encuesta de Presupuestos Familiares, Metodología y Resultados (Madrid, 1975).

[2] The 1970 census registered 34,040,641 inhabitants in Spain on 31 December 1970. A municipal count arrived at a figure of 36,025,784 for 31 December 1975. The 1970 census put the total number of families at 8,853,660 on 31 December 1970.

[3] Instituto Nacional de Estadística: Contabilidad Nacional de España base 1970 (Madrid, 1980), pp. 120-121 and pp. 308-309.

[4] With many thanks to the National Institute of Statistics.

Appendix 16.1: Household available income (pesetas/year) and number of households by household available income and household size, Spain, 1973

Household available income (pesetas/year) ('000)		Household size					
		1	2	3	4	5+	Total
- 60	a	35.5	43.7	43.4	46.5	44.9	39.6
	b	927	699	109	57	43	1 835
60- 84	a	70.6	72.0	73.3	72.4	73.5	72.1
	b	280	755	218	141	135	1 529
84-120	a	99.4	100.8	104.0	105.2	105.3	103.0
	b	268	1 010	600	496	633	3 007
120-180	a	147.8	147.0	151.1	153.2	153.1	151.2
	b	195	1 124	1 290	1 327	1 522	5 457
180-240	a	200.2	207.7	208.8	210.2	209.7	209.1
	b	100	633	1 055	1 202	1 479	4 469
240-480	a	308.0	318.3	313.2	321.8	329.3	322.8
	b	95	553	1 195	1 813	2 755	6 411
480-700	a	592.0	555.3	567.1	567.9	555.5	560.7
	b	18	82	143	224	531	998
700-	a	1 024.6	996.8	985.6	1 003.0	1 037.9	1 020.2
	b	8	37	60	86	254	445
Total	a	92.3	151.2	216.9	247.1	283.3	219.8
	b	1 891	4 892	4 672	5 346	7 351	24 151

a: household available income (pesetas per year).
b: number of households (estimated).

Source: National Institute of Statistics.

17. <u>SUDAN</u> (1967-68)

(S. Kansal, World Bank, Washington, DC)

Summary

The Sudanese income distribution estimates are based on the 1967-68 Household Sample Survey.[1] The income concept used in the survey was gross available household income, i.e. before tax. The survey did not include the population of the three southern provinces, but with the help of National Accounts data and the 1974 household survey (covering rural areas in the south) it was possible to include this part of the population as well. The study estimated the distributions of gross available income per household for urban, semi-urban and rural areas and for the country as a whole.

1. The 1967-68 Household Sample
    Survey

The 1967-68 survey covered the settled population of the six northern provinces of the country.[2] The three southern provinces - Equatoria, Bahr El Ghazal and Upper Nile - had to be left out because of politically unstable conditions.

For the survey, the six northern provinces of the country were divided into urban, semi-urban and rural areas.[3] The survey sample included a total of 7,080 households: 3,300 were urban, 780 semi-urban and 3,000 rural. The sampling fraction for the urban areas was 2 per cent, whereas for the rural areas it was 0.50 per cent for some selected areas and 0.25 per cent for the remaining ones. The survey report did not give the sampling fraction for the semi-urban areas.

The sampling frame for the urban and semi-urban areas was the 1964-65 population and housing survey, while for the rural areas it was the 1963 Census of Agriculture.

The survey followed a two-stage sampling procedure. In the first stage, 26 towns in the semi-urban areas and 300 sheikhdoms in the rural areas were selected with a probability proportionate to size (size being the number of households). For the urban areas, all 11 cities were included. In the second stage, households were selected by following a stratified sampling method, the strata being the deciles of households arranged in ascending order of income. In each area, the sample households were allocated in the ratio of 1:2:2 to the first three deciles, the next four deciles and the highest three deciles respectively.

The reference period for the survey was June 1967 to June 1968. Each household was interviewed 13 times. In the first interview, information was obtained on the socio-economic characteristics of the household. Data on income and expenditures were collected from the heads of households in 12 subsequent interviews, each covering a period of one month. The figures were tabulated to show annual average household income and expenditures for the year ending June 1968.

The survey report did not explicitly define the household. Indirect evidence showed that the survey included all persons living together as members of a household. The survey also covered one-person households.

Household income was taken as the sum of the income of all household members. It included monetary as well as non-monetary income from all sources, such as agriculture, animal husbandry, wages and salaries, business activities, etc. Also included were home-produced goods consumed by the households. The report did not mention whether the imputed income from owner-occupied houses was included or excluded. It was probably included under the income from other sources.

2. Evaluation of the 1967-68 survey

(a) Undercoverage

The 1967-68 survey covered the settled population of the six northern provinces of the country while the three southern provinces had to be left out. To assess the magnitude of the undercoverage, in this study the 1967-68 population and households were estimated using population census data from 1955-56 and 1973 (table 17.1).

The survey covered about 8.5 million settled population in the six northern provinces, who accounted for two-thirds of the total population.

In addition to the non-coverage of the population in the three southern provinces, the survey excluded the nomadic population of the northern rural areas, who accounted for about 12 per cent of total population. Because of their mobile existence, it is practically impossible to get income and expenditure data for nomads through a household survey. However, an attempt was made here to include the population of the three southern provinces in deriving the income distribution.

Table 17.1: Estimates of population and households, Sudan, 1967-68 (in thousands)

	Northern provinces		Southern provinces		Total	
	Popula-tion	House-holds	Popula-tion	House-holds	Popula-tion	House-holds
1. Urban	1 620	293	170	32	1 790	325
2. Rural, settled	6 880	1 410	2 680	474	9 560	1 884
3. Rural, nomads	1 610	322	-	-	1 610	322
4. Total, settled (1 + 2)	8 500	1 703	2 850	506	11 350	2 209
5. Total (3 + 4)	10 110	2 025	2 850	506	12 960	2 531

(b) Comparison with National Accounts

Normally it is possible to check broadly the reliability of the survey estimates of household income with similar figures derived from the National Accounts. In the case of the Sudan, however, this was not possible, as the survey covered only the settled population of the six northern provinces, while the National Accounts statistics cover the entire country.

The excluded population – the nomads and the population of the three southern provinces - live mostly in rural areas and are below the subsistence level. Thus the survey estimate of average household income is expected to be well above the national average derived from the National Accounts. Table 17.2 gives the estimates of average household income derived from the National Accounts statistics and the survey data.

The survey data for the six northern provinces showed an average household income of 189 S. pounds, which was about 6 per cent higher than the average income derived from the National Accounts data (177 S. pounds). After adjusting the survey data to include the southern area households, the adjusted average household income for the Sudan worked out to be 158 S. pounds - about 10 per cent lower than the National Accounts figure (see next section).

Table 17.2: <u>Average household income, Sudan, 1967-68 (in million Sudanese pounds)</u>

National Accounts	1967	1968	1967-68
1. National disposable income	495.6	540.7	518.2
2. Private consumption expenditures	413.8	443.6	428.7
3. Government consumption expenditures	63.1	77.5	70.3
4. Savings[1]	18.7	19.6	19.2
5. Household income (2 + 4)	432.5	463.2	447.9
6. Estimated households (millions)			2.53
7. Average household income (S. pounds)			177.0
Survey data:			
8. Average household income, unadjusted (S. pounds)			188.9
9. Average household income, adjusted (S. pounds)			158.0

[1] Savings are assumed to be household savings.

Source: Ministry of Planning, Department of Statistics: <u>The National Accounts and supporting tables, 1968</u> (Khartoum, July 1970), p. 18; tables 1 and 3 of the text.

3. <u>Data adjustment and the derivation of income distribution</u>

In 1974 the ILO[4] conducted a survey which covered the rural areas of the south. Although the results for household income were not very satisfactory, they did throw some light on household income levels. One of the findings was that in ten out of 12 villages in the south, all households had incomes below 50 S. pounds. In contrast, in only three out of 52 villages surveyed in the north did all the households report their income at below 50 S. pounds. The remaining two southern villages reported that all households had incomes below 100 S. pounds.

Keeping in mind that the survey data on income were not satisfactory and that own-produced consumption might have been under-reported, it was assumed that all the southern rural households had incomes below 200 S. pounds. They were therefore distributed in the three lowest income classes - below 50, 50 to 100 and 100 to 200 - in a ratio of 50:40:10, respectively.

For the urban areas in the south, it was assumed that the household distribution followed the same pattern as was observed in the semi-urban areas of northern Sudan.

Table 17.3: Distribution of adjusted gross household income (in percentages) Sudan, 1967-68

Deciles (households)	Urban	Semi-urban	Rural	Combined
I	2.0	1.3	1.8	1.2
II	3.2	3.1	3.0	2.8
III	5.0	4.8	4.2	4.0
IV	5.6	5.8	5.5	5.0
V	6.4	7.4	7.5	6.5
VI	7.8	7.6	9.0	8.5
VII	9.5	9.5	10.0	10.0
VIII	11.0	11.7	13.4	12.5
IX	16.0	16.3	17.1	14.9
X	33.5	32.5	28.5	34.6
Gini index	0.41	0.41	0.38	0.44

Another adjustment was made to the original survey data. It had been observed that in the survey the lowest income class (below 100) had contained a large proportion of rural households. If the rural households of the south were added to those of the survey, for the whole country the lowest class would contain about 50 per cent of all rural households. Thus the households in the lowest income class were subdivided into two income groups - below 50 and 50 to 100 S. pounds - in such a way that the average household income for all households reported in the survey remained unaltered.

The adjusted decile distributions of households for urban, semi-urban and rural areas of the Sudan are given in table 17.3.

Notes

[1] Ministry of Planning, Department of Statistics: Household sample survey in the Sudan, 1967-68 (Khartoum, Dec. 1970).

[2] In 1967-68 the Sudan was administratively divided into nine provinces - Northern, Khartoum, Kassala, Blue Nile, Kordofan, Darfur, Equatoria, Bahr El Ghazal and Upper Nile.

[3] All cities with a population of 35,000 or more were taken as urban. The semi-urban areas comprised the 70 smaller towns which had been included in the 1964-65 population and housing survey. All the remaining areas, which consisted of a large number of sheikhdoms, were treated as rural.

[4] ILO: Growth, employment and equity: A comprehensive strategy for the the Sudan (Geneva, 1976), Technical Papers 9 and 10.

Appendix 17.1: Gross household income distribution by income class
(unadjusted), Sudan, 1967-68 (six northern provinces)

Annual income class (S. pounds)	Urban	Semi-urban	Rural
Below 50	1.3	7.8	17.1
50- 100	2.6	7.8	17.1
100- 200	24.2	34.0	47.7
200- 300	24.8	22.3	11.1
300- 400	14.6	11.8	4.3
400- 500	9.6	5.8	1.4
500- 600	6.2	3.3	0.4
600- 700	4.2	2.1	0.4
700- 800	3.0	1.3	0.1
800- 900	2.3	0.7	0.2
900-1 000	1.5	0.6	0.1
1 000-1 200	2.1	1.6	0.1
1 200-1 500	1.6	0.4	0.0
1 500 and above	2.2	0.5	0.1
All households	100.0	100.0	100.0
Average household income (S. pounds)	410.7	269.6	148.0

Source: Ministry of Planning, Development of Statistics: Household
sample survey, 1967-68 (Khartoum, Dec. 1970).

18. SWEDEN (1979)

(W. van Ginneken, ILO, Geneva)

Summary

The Swedish income distribution estimates are based on the 1979 Income Distribution Survey. The income concept used by the survey is household available income. The household concept is different from that in other countries. It considers any adult (person more than 18 years old) who is not married or not cohabiting, as a one-person household, even if he or she lives in with his or her family. For each source of income, the survey data were adjusted to the corresponding National Accounts totals. Capital income was adjusted in proportion to measured capital income (and not allocated to the highest quintile) because in Sweden low-income classes (in particular pensioners) derive a high proportion of their income from capital. The study estimated the distributions of available income per household and per head.

1. Introduction

The income distribution estimates in this chapter are based on the 1979 Income Distribution Survey carried out by the National Central Bureau of Statistics. The survey covers all groups of households except institutional ones. The annual sample consists of about 27,000 individuals, constituting about 10,000 households, and is selected from a computer register including the whole population. A mail survey is then undertaken between January and April in the year following the income year. In May a computer register is established, covering all the persons in the households of the selected individuals. This register is then used as the basis for the collection of data on income, social benefits, etc. which are collected from September to December. The sources of information on income include tax returns, which are obtained from local taxation authorities, sickness allowance, housing allowance and social assistance obtained from government insurance offices, social benefit bureaux and other authorities.

The household concept used in the survey is narrower than the one used in most other countries. The household is defined as either two adults who have lived, or normally should have lived, at least half the income year in the same dwelling, irrespective of marital status and with or without children. Adults are considered to be persons 18 years of age or more and younger persons who are married. As a result of this definition, any adult who is not married or is not cohabiting is considered as a single-person household, even if he or she lives in with his or her family.

The <u>income concept</u> employed is household available income, which
is the sum of wages and salaries (excluding social security
contributions), net entrepreneurial income, income from capital,
imputed rent from owner-occupied housing and transfers minus direct
income and capital taxes, and other than social security contributions.

2.   Consistency with National Accounts

As is usually the case, the aggregated incomes of the survey
underestimate the corresponding National Accounts totals, and table
18.1 shows to what extent this is the case.

Table 18.1: Disposable income from the 1979 survey compared with
National Accounts data (in million kroner)

	1979 survey (1)	National Accounts (2)	100* (1):(2)
Wages and salaries (excl. social security contributions)	219 261	219 068	100.0
Net entrepreneurial income	12 982	16 262	79.8
Income from capital	4 743	11 755	40.3
Imputed rent from owner-occupied housing	21 003	16 399	128.1
Transfer income	80 224	94 613	84.8
Direct income and capital taxes	95 825	99 428	96.4
Other than social security contributions	1 045	10 124	10.3
Total	241 343	248 545	97.1

It shows that most income sources as measured by the 1979 survey are fairly close to the 1979 National Accounts data. Two exceptions are two relatively small sources of income: income from capital that is only captured for about 40 per cent, and "other than social security contributions" where this percentage is only 10 per cent. Imputed rent from owner-occupied housing - as measured by the survey - is about 30 per cent higher than the amount estimated by National Accounts. It is reasonable to assume that the survey captures this item better than National Accounts, and as a result the survey data referring to this item were not adjusted to the National Accounts total. Another change that we made in the adjustments concerns income from capital. In all other country studies we adjusted income from capital only for the highest quintile of households. In the case of Sweden, this would have led to unacceptable results because the percentage of capital income in total disposable income in the highest quintile varies between 0.1 and 2.0 per cent, while it is relatively high (about 20 per cent) in the lowest decile.[1] As a result, we decided to apply a proportional adjustment to capital income, as was done for the other sources of income.

3. The household data

As explained in section 1, the Swedish definition of household is more restricted than the one employed in most other countries. As table 18.2 shows, there is a relatively high percentage of single-person households. Table 18.2 further shows that we did not have available the distribution of households according to size but according to household type.

4. Results

Table 18.3 shows the main results for Sweden. The estimates are based on tables which cross-classify households according to household disposable income (20 income classes) and seven household types of different size (see table 18.2). Since the income distribution survey does not include information on household food expenditure, we were not able to estimate the economies-of-scale factor as was done for some other countries.

Unlike most other industrialised countries, the inequality of per head distribution is much lower than that of the per household distribution. This is due to the high percentage of single-person households. To some extent, this difference is artificial, because a considerable part of the "single-person households" are single persons older than 18 years but who still live with their families.

Table 18.2: The distribution of households by household type (in numbers and percentages)

	Households		Persons	
	Number	Percentage	Number	Percentage
Single persons	2 127 616	49.6	2 127 616	26.1
Single person + 1 child	122 075	2.8	244 150	3.0
Single person + 2 children or more	68 538	1.6	220 346	2.9
Married/cohabitant couple	1 056 213	24.6	2 112 426	25.9
Couple + 1 child	361 504	8.4	1 084 512	13.3
Couple + 2 children	419 248	9.8	1 676 992	20.5
Couple + 3 children or more	132 952	3.1	697 384	8.5
Total	4 288 146	100.0	8 163 426	100.0

Table 18.3: Distribution of household available income (in percentages); original data and data adjusted with National Accounts, Sweden, 1979

Type of data	Original		Adjusted	
Income concept	I	II	I	II
Recipient unit	Household	Person	Household	Person
Deciles				
I	2.3	3.4	2.6	3.5
II	4.0	6.0	4.6	6.0
III	5.7	7.2	6.1	7.1
IV	6.6	8.0	6.7	8.3
V	7.9	8.8	7.5	9.1
VI	9.2	9.6	9.9	10.1
VII	11.4	11.1	11.8	11.4
VIII	13.9	12.3	13.6	12.4
IX	16.6	14.4	16.0	13.5
X	22.3	19.1	21.2	18.5
Gini index	0.33	0.24	0.30	0.22

It is further noteworthy that - unlike all other countries - the adjusted distribution is more equal than the estimate based on the original distribution. This is explained by the facts (see section 2) that we adjusted capital income proportionally and that a relatively large part of underestimated income refers to transfer income which is concentrated in the lower income classes.

Note

[1] This is due to the fact that the majority of persons in the lowest quintile are pensioners, who have a comparatively high percentage of their income in capital income.

19. TANZANIA (1969)

(E. Beverly Downes, Monash University,
Victoria, Australia)

Summary

The Tanzanian income distribution estimate is based on the 1969
Household Budget Survey.   The income concept used by the survey was
cash income.   On the basis of the consumption expenditure data of the
survey and the corresponding National Accounts data, it was possible
to estimate adjusted non-monetary income for each income class.   The
estimates of current household savings were derived from the survey
data on financial savings and adjusted to the corresponding National
Accounts total.   The study generated the national distribution of
available income per household.

1.   Data source

The basic source for deriving household income distribution in
Tanzania is the 1969 Household Budget Survey (HBS), conducted by the
Bureau of Statistics of Tanzania.   Although the 1976-77 HBS has also
been completed, all the results were not available at the time of
writing.   However, it is possible to derive estimates of cash income
for 1975 from the listing of households from the 1976-77 HBS.

2.   Brief description of the 1969 survey

This survey covered all private households in both the rural and
the urban areas of mainland Tanzania.   The sample contained 4,092
households, or about 0.15 per cent of the total in the country.   Of
those, 2,232 households were from the rural areas (representing about
0.09 per cent of total rural households), and 1,860 were from the
urban areas (about 1.2 per cent of total urban households).

The survey was conducted during the calendar year 1969.   The
reference period for rural areas and small towns was one month.   For
Dar es Salaam, it was ten days for cash income and food expenditures,
and ten days to ten months for non-food expenditures.   The tabulated
results gave annualised figures for 1969.

A household was defined as a single person or a group of persons
(except where there were more than five boarders or lodgers) living
together and sharing expenditures.   Household income covered only
cash income and excluded all income in kind.

Table 19.1: Private consumption expenditure coverage in the 1969 survey compared to that in the National Accounts, mainland Tanzania

| | Millions of shillings | | Per cent covered by survey |
	1969 National Accounts (1)	1969 Survey (2)	100*(2):(1)
Food, beverages and tobacco	3 216	2 782	86.5
Clothing and footwear	453	492	108.6
Gross rent and water charges	735	67	9.1
Miscellaneous*	1 425	830	58.2
Private consumption expenditure	5 829	4 171	71.6

(1) Economic Affairs and Development Planning: National Accounts of Tanzania, 1964-72 (Dar es Salaam, 1974), p. 32, table 23.

(2) 1969 household budget survey, Vol. 1, Appendix 8.1:a.

* Including fuel and power, furniture, furnishings, household equipment and domestic services, medical care and health expenses, transport and communication, recreation, entertainment and educational services, other services and net expenditure abroad by resident households.

The 1969 survey gave an itemised distribution of household consumption expenditures by consumption expenditure classes. The survey definition of consumption expenditures included cash as well as non-cash items valued at market prices. It also included monetary outlays on non-consumption items such as taxes, financial savings, investments and transfers.

Table 19.2: Distribution of adjusted household available income (in percentages), mainland Tanzania, 1969

Deciles (households)

I	2.1
II	3.7
III	4.9
IV	5.3
V	6.4
VI	7.5
VII	8.9
VIII	10.8
IX	14.8
X	35.6
Gini index	0.42

3. Evaluation of the 1969 survey

Data were collected from 3,068 sample households out of the total of 4,092, giving a high rate of non-enumeration (about 25 per cent).[1] Within rural areas and small towns, almost all the sample households were covered (2,196 out of the planned 2,232 sample households). However, in Dar es Salaam only about half the sample households were covered (872 out of 1,860).

The survey covered only cash income and omitted all non-cash income. It estimated total income of 3,545 million shillings equalled 55 per cent of the total disposable income derived from the National Accounts (6,439 million shillings). As non-cash income constitutes a higher percentage of total income for the lower income classes, its omission has produced a distribution which is strongly biased.

Total household consumption expenditures as derived from the survey (4,171 million shillings) equalled 71.6 per cent of the private consumption expenditure derived from the National Accounts (5,829 million shillings). Thus, the survey appears to have under-reported expenditures by about 28.4 per cent (see table 19.1).

Although the survey was to be conducted over the whole of 1969, in order to speed up publication of the results the annual estimates were based on data for seven months (for Dar es Salaam data for only six months were used). By not fully taking into account seasonal factors, this decision undoubtedly introduced a bias in estimating cash income and consumption data, especially in rural areas where 31 per cent of cash income was from crops.

4. Derivation of income distribution

The distribution of disposable household income can be derived from the survey data on the consumption expenditures of households. In the survey, consumption expenditures were defined as the sum of cash and non-cash outlays valued at market prices and included monetary transactions on such items as taxes, savings, investments and transfers.[2]

To estimate the distribution of total disposable household income, several adjustments were made to the survey data on the distribution of household consumption expenditures. First, expenditures on non-consumption items were excluded. Second, the itemised consumption expenditures were inflated to equal the National Accounts levels to adjust for under-reporting. Third, the estimates of current household savings were derived from the survey data on financial savings by netting out such non-current income as proceeds from the sale of assets, and then by inflating the results to equal the estimates of private savings derived from the National Accounts. Finally, the distribution of total disposable household income was derived by adding the adjusted distributions of private consumption expenditures and private savings. Table 19.2 shows the adjusted income distribution by deciles of households and the gini index for mainland Tanzania (the adjustments are shown in the appendix).

Notes

[1] Non-enumeration includes non-response. Other reasons for non-enumeration could either be a vacant house or the inability of the enumerator to contact the sample household.

[2] According to the Bureau of Statistics introduction to the National Accounts of Tanzania 1964-72, the consumption expenditure data from the 1969 survey represented "total income inclusive of subsistence production".

Appendix 19.1: Total household disposable income derived from consumption expenditure in the 1969 survey, mainland Tanzania (thousands of shillings)

	Average household expenditure groups (shillings)								
	0 to 999	1 000 to 1 999	2 000 to 3 999	4 000 to 5 999	6 000 to 7 999	8 000 to 9 999	10 000 to 24 999	25 000 and over	All classes
1. Private consumption expenditure (excl. non-consumption items)	545 457	1 368 860	1 158 337	476 745	248 315	70 589	203 275	99 578	4 171 156
2. Adjustments to national accounts levels	140 543	357 798	389 038	223 416	137 882	63 931	241 597	103 795	1 658 000
2.1 Food, beverages and tobacco	71 610	170 562	123 256	43 400	15 624	3 038	5 642	868	434 000
2.2 Clothing and footwear	-4 095	-12 129	-12 363	-4 641	-2 808	-585	-1 638	-741	-39 000
2.3 Gross rent and water charges	4 008	16 700	116 900	116 232	88 176	50 768	197 728	77 488	668 000
2.4 Miscellaneous	69 020	182 665	161 245	68 425	36 890	10 710	39 865	26 180	595 000
3. Adjusted private consumption expenditure (excl. non-consumption items) (1+2)	686 000	1 726 658	1 547 375	700 161	386 197	134 520	444 872	203 373	5 829 156
4. Financial savings	32 821	128 615	256 384	156 575	109 797	73 530	143 323	118 855	1 019 900
5. Less "Sale of assets"	22 214	29 355	19 722	6 604	2 585	929	1 587	475	83 471
6. Private savings (4-5)	10 607	99 260	236 662	149 971	107 212	72 601	141 736	118 380	936 429
7. Adjusted to national accounts private savings	6 710	64 660	154 330	97 600	70 150	47 580	92 110	76 860	610 000
8. Net total disposable income (3+7)	692 710	1 791 318	1 701 705	797 761	456 347	182 100	536 982	280 233	6 439 156

Source: Rows 1 and 4: Ministry of Economic Affairs and Development Planning, Bureau of Statistics: 1969 household budget survey - Volume 1: Income and consumption (Dar es Salaam, 1972), Appendix 8.1:2.

Rows 2, 5 and 7 are described in the text.

20. TRINIDAD AND TOBAGO (1975-76)

(J.-G. Park, World Bank, Washington, DC)

Summary

The income distribution estimate for Trinidad and Tobago is based
on the 1975-76 Household Budget Survey. The income concept used by
the survey is cash income.   On the basis of survey data on
consumption expenditure, the income data were adjusted.   No full
adjustment with National Accounts was, however, achieved.   The study
estimated the distribution of available income per household for the
years 1971-72 and 1975-76.

The National Household Budget Surveys (HBS) carried out by the
country's Central Statistical Office are the primary sources for
estimating household income distribution in Trinidad and Tobago.   The
1975-76 HBS was the third such national sample survey.   The two
previous ones were conducted in 1957-58 and 1971-72.   This chapter
provides household income distribution estimates for 1975-76 and
compares these with similar estimates for 1971-72.

1. Brief description of the
    1975-76 survey

The survey covered all private households except institutional
households constituting hostels, boarding houses and prisons.   The
sample consisted of 2,992 households, representing 1.2 per cent of all
private households in the country in 1975.   The sampling frame was
the same as that used in the 1970 census, but was updated to reflect
population changes and new housing areas.

The survey was conducted in two rounds of six months each.   The
first ran from mid-March to mid-September 1975, the second from
October 1975 to March 1976.   Information was collected partly by
interview and partly by records kept by individual spenders in the
households.[1] The reference period for data on income was either the
previous one month or the most recent pay period.

A household was defined as comprising one or more persons,
related or unrelated, who occupied the same dwelling, slept most
nights there and shared at least one meal daily.   Household income
was defined as the sum of money income of all household members before
deductions for income tax, insurance and contributions to pension
funds, etc.   It included such transfers as pensions and gifts, but
excluded income in kind, the imputed value of owner-occupied dwellings
and production consumed by the producer.

2. Evaluation of the 1975-76 survey

Of the total sample of 2,992 households, information was actually collected for only 2,493 households, resulting in a high rate of non-enumeration (including non-response) of 16.7 per cent. Comparison of the data on the distribution of sample households and the average household income by major administrative areas showed that areas with high average household income were under-represented in the actual sample, whereas areas with low income were over-represented. This indicates that the sample was biased towards the lower-income households.

The survey data showed that average expenditures exceeded average incomes (including imputed incomes) for all but two income classes. The under-reporting of income was particularly pronounced for the lowest income class. For these households, average expenditures were more than three times the average reported incomes. For the country as a whole, average household expenditures exceeded average household income, indicating negative savings by the household sector as a whole. The reason for such an anomaly appears to be that most sample households under-reported their income in the survey.

A comparison of total household income as derived from the survey with estimates of private consumption expenditures from the National Accounts showed that the former was 54 per cent of the latter. Even when the survey estimates were adjusted upward by including such non-monetary income as imputed rents and home-grown consumption, this proportion increased to only 60 per cent (see appendix).

3. Derivation of income distribution

The survey data on income were adjusted upward by adding imputed rent from owner-occupied dwellings and the value of home-grown food consumption expenditures.

To adjust the survey data for the under-reporting of income, it was first assumed that for those households which reported incomes lower than expenditures, actual incomes were equal to reported expenditures. These households were then reclassified into higher income classes. Total household income as derived from the adjusted data was 55 per cent higher than that estimated from the original data. Table 1 gives both income distribution by deciles of household and the gini index.

Table 20.1:   Distribution of adjusted household available income (in percentages), Trinidad and Tobago, 1971-72 and 1975-76

Deciles (households)	1971-72	1975-76
I	1.5	1.6
II	2.3	2.6
III	4.1	3.8
IV	5.4	5.3
V	6.2	6.5
VI	8.9	7.4
VII	9.7	9.5
VIII	12.1	13.3
IX	16.9	18.2
X	32.9	31.8
Gini index	0.45	0.45

4.   Comparison over time

A review of the 1971-72 household budget survey indicated that household income was also generally under-reported and that, for many income classes, average household expenditures exceeded average incomes.   Using similar assumptions as were used for adjusting the 1975-76 survey results, adjusted estimates were derived for 1971-72 household income distribution.   Table 20.1 gives the income distribution by deciles of households for 1971-72.

A comparison of the household income distribution estimates for 1971-72 and 1975-76 showed that the pattern of distribution remained virtually unchanged over the period.

5. Concluding remarks

Despite their national coverage, the published 1975-76 survey data results did not provide separate estimates for rural and urban areas. No information on income distribution by household members was published. Furthermore, other relevant independent data sources (e.g. census and National Accounts data) did not provide sufficient information for a full evaluation of the survey data.

Note

[1] Spenders were defined as household members who were 18 or more years of age or who were under 18 but working and not attending an educational institution on a full-time basis. Persons 65 or more years of age and not heads of households were excluded from the list of spenders.

Appendix 20.1: Derivation of adjusted available household income per monthly monetary income class (in pesos), Trinidad and Tobago, 1975-76

Monthly monetary income class	Average monetary income (A)	Imputed rents[1] (B)	Home-grown food[1] (C)	Adjusted average monthly income (A+B+C)
0- 49	20.5	31.9	8.1	60.5
50- 99	71.7	33.9	9.6	115.2
100- 199	147.8	33.5	10.6	191.9
200- 299	247.5	46.5	13.5	307.5
300- 499	388.6	57.9	13.4	459.9
500- 699	582.3	81.0	12.1	675.4
700- 899	783.3	118.0	14.6	915.9
900-1 099	988.3	161.4	12.3	1 162.0
1 100-1 299	1 200.7	172.6	9.4	1 382.7
1 300-1 499	1 376.4	223.2	11.3	1 610.9
1 500+	2 017.4	387.4	7.8	2 412.6
National average	457.5	78.2	11.9	547.6

[1] Derived from HBS data on household expenditures.

Source: Household budgetary survey, 1975-76, Bulletin No. 1, op. cit., table 1B, p. 1 and Household budgetary survey, 1975-76, Report No. 2, op. cit., table 26, pp. 22-27.

21. <u>UNITED KINGDOM</u> (1979)

(W. van Ginneken, ILO, Geneva)

Summary

The income distribution estimates for the United Kingdom are based on the 1979 Family Expenditure Survey.[1] The income concept used in the survey is household available income. For each type of income, survey data were adjusted for inconsistency with National Accounts totals. The study generated the distributions of available income per household, per head and per equivalent unit.

1. Introduction

The data source used for estimating the distribution of income in this chapter is the 1979 Family Expenditure Survey. It provides information on household available income and the household is considered as the central income (spending) unit. Using the Family Expenditure Survey has also its disadvantages. About 30 per cent of the households included in the effective sample do not normally co-operate. A study made on the 1971 sample found substantial response variations; households without children and those where the head was, or had been, self-employed produced lower response rates.[2] It is also mentioned in the survey that "certain forms of income, such as income from investment, occupational pensions, or self-employment, are believed to be underestimated"[3] and that "the main identified weaknesses in the survey were found to be an understatement of earnings by women in part-time employment, and an under-representation of the highest 1 per cent of earners".[4] Since this chapter attempts to adjust the survey data for inconsistencies with National Accounts, it will be able partly to correct for these biases.

2. Concepts and methodology

The household concept used in the Family Expenditure Survey is well comparable with that employed in other countries. It "comprises one person living alone or a group of people living at the same address having meals prepared together and with common housekeeping".[5]

The information available for estimating the per head distribution is a table cross-classifying households by household gross income and household size. It is therefore important to know whether the distribution of household size in the sample of 6,777 households corresponds with that of more reliable population

estimates.   The 1979 edition of <u>Social Trends</u> projects the average
household size for England and Wales at 2.70, which corresponds
exactly with the value found in the 1979 Family Expenditure
Survey.[6]   Moreover, the distribution published in the 1979 Family
Expenditure Survey seems to follow naturally the trend towards more
small households.   There is therefore no need to adjust the sample
weights of the 1979 FES data.

However, one type of adjustment that is needed is to make them
consistent with National Accounts, which are generally considered to
be more reliable.   Table 21.1 shows to what extent the 1979 Family
Expenditure Survey underestimates the corresponding totals of the
National Accounts.

As is commonly observed both in developed and in developing
countries, the aggregate household survey estimates are lower than the
corresponding totals of National Accounts.   The underestimation is
highest for net income from self-employment, investments and
occupational pensions.

With the data adjusted for National Accounts, we also estimated
the following double-log food expenditure functions:

$$\text{Log } F \quad = 1.252 + \underset{(0.002)}{0.426 \text{ log } Y} \quad + \underset{(0.002)}{0.497 \text{ log } N} \qquad \begin{array}{l} R^2 = 0.98 \\ e = 0.866 \end{array}$$

$$\text{Log } (F/N) = 1.267 + \underset{(0.001)}{0.424 \text{ log } (Y/N)} - \underset{(0.001)}{0.099 \text{ log } N} \qquad \begin{array}{l} R^2 = 0.93 \\ e = 0.828 \end{array}$$

The economies-of-scale factor (0.866) was used for estimating
household available income per equivalent unit as shown in the next
section.

2.   Results

Table 21.2 shows the result of the adjustments for National
Accounts, both for the per household and the per head distribution of
household available income.

There is little difference between the distributions which are
adjusted or not for inconsistencies with National Accounts.   On the
other hand, there is a substantial difference in inequality between
the per household on the one hand and per head and per equivalent unit
distribution of income on the other hand (I, II and III in table
21.2).   The inequality of the per head and per equivalent unit
distributions is significantly lower.

Table 21.1: Estimates of various income items according to National Accounts and the 1979 Family Expenditure Survey (in million pounds), United Kingdom, 1979

	National Accounts Survey (1)	1979 Family Expenditure (2)	100* (2):(1) = (3)
Usual wages and salaries	98 511[1]	93 016	94.4
Net income from self-employment	12 848[2]	6 438	50.1
Investment income	5 577[3]	3 568	64.0
Income from occupational pensions	4 744[4]	3 395	71.6
State benefits	20 066[5]	16 935	84.4
Other income (incl. imputed rent)	10 763[6]	7 453	69.2
Gross normal income	152 509	130 805	85.8
Direct taxes and national insurance contributions of employers and self-employed	26 455[7]	22 359	84.5
Superannuation and all insurance premiums	5 834	4 513	77.4
Available household income	120 220	103 933	86.5

[1] Includes wages and salaries plus pay in cash of H.M. Forces (table 4.4).

[2] Equals income from self-employment after providing for depreciation and stock appreciation (table 4.3).

[3] Equals gross receipts of rent, dividends and interest less interest paid plus depreciation and stock appreciation of income from self-employment.

[4] Equals occupational pension and estimated benefits from superannuation schemes.

[5] Includes some receipts from private non-profit-making bodies (table 4.4).

[6] Includes rent of owner-occupied dwellings, income in kind and benefit from life assurance benefits (table 4.4).

[7] Taxes on income and additions to taxes plus social security contributions less employers' contributions.

Source: National Accounts: Central Statistical Office: National income and expenditure, 1980, London, HMSO, 1980.

Table 21.2: Distribution of household available income (in percentages), per household, per head and per equivalent unit; original data and data adjusted for National Accounts, United Kingdom, 1979

Type of data	Original data			Adjusted for National Accounts		
Income concept*	I	II	III	I	II	III
Recipient unit	House-hold (1)	Person (2)	Person (3)	House-hold (4)	Person (5)	Person (6)
Deciles						
I	2.9	3.9	4.1	2.8	3.9	4.2
II	4.1	5.6	5.7	4.5	5.6	5.7
III	5.4	6.4	6.5	5.5	6.3	6.5
IV	6.9	7.2	7.3	6.9	7.2	7.2
V	8.4	8.1	8.2	8.2	8.0	8.1
VI	9.9	9.3	9.3	9.5	9.1	9.1
VII	11.4	10.4	10.7	10.9	10.5	10.5
VIII	13.1	12.3	12.4	12.5	12.0	12.1
IX	15.6	15.2	14.9	15.5	14.8	14.5
X	22.4	21.5	20.7	23.8	22.6	22.0
Gini index	0.31	0.27	0.25	0.32	0.27	0.26

* I: household available income;
 II: household available income per head;
 III: household available income per equivalent unit.

The difference between the adjusted and unadjusted distributions is small because aggregated household available income underestimates the corresponding National Accounts total by only 15 per cent. Moreover, since the adjustment for investment income - which is attributed to the highest quintile of households - is relatively small (i.e. about 2 per cent of total available income), it is only having a small impact on the highest income classes.

Notes

[1] Department of Employment: Family expenditure survey, 1979 (London, HMSO, 1980).

[2] W.F.F. Kemsley: "Family expenditure survey - A study of differential response based on a comparison of the 1971 sample with the census", in Statistical News (London, HMSO), No. 31, Nov. 1975.

[3] Department of Employment, op. cit., p. 3.

[4] ibid., p. 3.

[5] ibid., p. 153.

[6] Central Statistical Office: Social trends, 1979 (London, HMSO, 1979).

22. YUGOSLAVIA (1978)

(J.-G. Park, World Bank, Washington, DC)

Summary

The Yugoslavian income distribution estimate is based on the 1979 Survey on Receipts, Expenditures and Consumption of Households.[1] The income concept used in the survey is gross available household income (i.e. before tax). Survey data on consumption expenditure and on savings were adjusted separately for inconsistencies with National Accounts. The study generated the distribution of gross available income per household.

The basic data source for the derivation of household income distribution in Yugoslavia for 1978 was the 1978 Anketa o Prihodima, Rashodima i Potrosnji Domacinstava (APRIPD or Survey on Receipts, Expenditures and Consumption of Households), carried out in 1978 by the Federal Institute of Statistics in co-operation with the statistical agencies in all republics of the country. To date, only preliminary results of the survey have been published.

1. Brief description of the 1978 survey

The survey covered all private households in the country, excluding institutional households such as boarding schools, nursing homes and hospitals. The sample size was 18,655 households, or 0.3 per cent of total private households. Interviews were conducted in December 1978, and the reference period was the calendar year 1978.

A household was defined as a single person or a group of persons living together and spending their income together. The survey included domestic workers living in the household. While household members who studied away from home were included as household members, boarders and lodgers were excluded. Household income was defined as before-tax income, which included all current receipts from employment as well as transfers. In addition, the imputed value of goods consumed out of production within the household, and such non-current "receipts" as proceeds from the sale of assets, insurance claims and consumer loans, were also included.

2. Evaluation of the 1978 survey

Information was obtained from 18,621 households out of the 18,655 households in the sample. Thus the non-enumeration rate (including non-response) was insignificant (0.2 per cent).

The stratification of areas for the sample selection in the 1978 survey was based on the 1971 population census. Considering the rate of urbanisation between 1971 and 1978, the sample for the 1978 survey may have been biased towards relatively fewer urban households. On the other hand, there is some evidence that the income distribution pattern in non-urban areas is not very different from that in urban areas. Thus, in terms of income distribution, the survey was not affected.

Household income in the survey included non-current items such as proceeds from the sale of assets, consumer loans, etc. Total consumer loans by households were significant (105,000 million dinars) compared to total current household income (629,000 million dinars). However, no data were available to distribute the amounts by income class.

A comparison of total household consumption expenditures as derived from the survey data and from the National Accounts showed that the former were about 89 per cent of the latter. There is some evidence to suggest that the survey under-reported household consumption expenditures, mainly in terms of "non-material" services.

3. Derivation of income distribution

The report published by the Federal Institute of Statistics does not provide data on the distribution of current household income, but it does include data on the distribution of household consumption expenditures and savings. The distribution of current household income was therefore derived by using the published estimates on expenditures and savings, since current income equals consumption expenditures plus savings.

A number of adjustments were made to the published series to obtain income distribution estimates. First, the survey data on household consumption expenditures were uniformly adjusted upward, so that the resulting aggregate value became equal to the corresponding National Accounts figure. Next, the aggregate household savings estimated from the National Accounts data (89,900 million dinars) were distributed across different income classes in proportion to the household savings as reported in the survey. Finally, by combining the distributions of adjusted household consumption expenditures and of household savings, an estimate of household income distribution was derived for Yugoslavia.[2] Table 22.1 gives the income distribution by deciles of households and the gini index.

Table 22.1: Distribution of household gross available income (in percentages), Yugoslavia, 1978

Deciles of households

I	2.4
II	4.2
III	5.4
IV	6.7
V	8.2
VI	9.4
VII	11.6
VIII	13.4
IX	15.8
X	22.9
Gini index	0.33

Table 22.2: Distribution of household gross available income by quintiles of households (in percentages), Yugoslavia, 1973 and 1978

Household groups	Percentage of household income	
	1973	1978
Lowest 20 per cent	6.5	6.6
2nd quintile	11.9	12.1
3rd quintile	17.6	18.7
4th quintile	24.0	23.9
Highest 20 per cent	40.0	38.7
Highest 10 per cent	22.5	22.9
Gini index	0.32	0.33

4. Comparison over time

Comparing the 1978 income distribution with that for 1973, it may be observed that the size distribution of household income in Yugoslavia remained virtually unchanged. Table 22.2 gives household income distributions for the two years by quintiles, along with the gini indices.

5. Concluding remarks

The distribution of household income in Yugoslavia for 1978 was estimated using the preliminary results of the country's latest national household survey. Household income, derived by adding consumption expenditures and savings, refers to the after-tax income of all household members accruing from all current income sources including the non-material service sectors.

Notes

[1] The 1978 survey was the fourth nation-wide household survey in Yugoslavia. Previous surveys were conducted in 1963, 1968 and 1973.

[2] Estimates are presented only at national level, as the relevant data for deriving rural-urban distributions were not available.

23. <u>ZAMBIA</u> (1976)

(R. van der Hoeven, ILO, Geneva)

Summary

The Zambian income distribution estimate is based on the 1976 household survey. The income concept used in the survey was household disposable income (i.e. excluding imputed rent). National Accounts totals for various income sources were available for four socio-economic groups. The corresponding survey data were adjusted for inconsistency with these totals. The study generated the distributions of disposable income per household for urban and rural areas and for the country as a whole.

1. Introduction

The income distribution estimate in this chapter is based on the 1976 survey which covered 1,004 urban and 794 rural households, and which took place between December 1975 and December 1976. At the time of the preparation of this chapter, the official publication had not yet been published. The estimates in this chapter are in fact based on some ad hoc tabulations of the so-called Turner report.[1]

The available tabulations from the 1976 survey include average household disposable income for four socio-economic groups: urban households in squatter areas, in low- and high-cost housing areas, and rural households. For each group there are tabulations on the distribution of disposable household incomes.[2] The income concept used by the survey includes net cash wages (i.e. after tax and employers' contributions), wages in kind, business profits and the consumption of own produce. The imputed value of owner-occupied housing does not seem to be included. The household concept corresponds to that recommended by the United Nations.

2. Consistency with National Accounts

In table 23.1 the survey results are compared with the National Accounts figures. Wages and salaries in the budget survey refer to the wages and salaries received by the families. Thus employers' contributions are not included, while contributions in kind are recorded under other income (which includes gifts). As most income tax is already deducted from the source (the so-called pay-as-you-earn scheme which accounts for almost all the income tax paid by the employed), the household budget survey under-reports total wage and salary income. The total amount of wages and salaries received in 1976 according to the regularly published employment and earnings survey[3] amounts to K695 million, to which should be added an estimated K17 million for wages of domestic servants, which brings the total wage income to K712 million.

Table 23.1: Sources of income, 1976 (K. million)

	Survey outcome			National Accounts
	Urban	Rural	Total	
Wages, etc.	554	110	664	886
Profits	9 (high-cost areas)	195	271	276
	67 (other)			
Other income	48	31	79	
Imputed value of own produce		143	143	178
Total	678	479	1 157	1 340

The National Accounts figure includes all wage costs (which are usually 20 per cent to 25 per cent of the paid wages). If we deduct from that the pay-as-you-earn taxes and the selective employment taxes, amounting to a total of K72 million, total wage and salary income amounts to K815 million which is 22 per cent or K150 million higher than the wages reported by the household budget survey.

The National Accounts do not publish separate figures on profits, so that these have to be derived indirectly. From the operating surplus (K623 million) the imputed value of own produce subsistence farming (K178 million) was first subtracted, then the profits transferred out of the country (K108 million), and finally the company tax from mining and non-mining activities (K66 million).

The resulting figures for profits (K271 million) closely resemble that of the budget survey. However, most profits earned by rich people are hardly reported in the survey (a meagre total of K9 million). The household budget survey thus reveals profits from transactions which are not or only partly covered by the National Accounts statistics. As the detailed National Accounts figures for 1976 have not yet been published, it is difficult to gauge the underestimation of profits of the rich in the household budget survey and the underestimation of the profits of the poor in the National Accounts figures.   A rough guess would be along the following lines.

The operating surplus of the commercial agricultural sector is estimated to be K27 million, which is supposed to be covered under the profits of the budget survey for the rural sector, and thus subtracted from the K271 million operating surplus of the National Accounts. This gives a figure of K243 million for urban areas, of which K76 million is accounted for, which means that the budget survey under-reports by an amount of K168 million.

The budget survey also under-reports the imputed value of own consumption by an amount of K36 million.

Table 23.2:   Adjustment of the income of the four strata of the 1976 household budget survey (K. million)

	Squatter areas	Low- cost housing areas	High- cost housing areas	Rural areas	Total
Total income according to HBS (K. million)	132	326	219	479	1 157
Adjustment for wage income	19	60	46	25	150
Adjustment for distributed profits			168		168
Adjustment for imputed value of own produce				36	37
Total	151	387	433	539	

3.   Estimate of the national
      income distribution

The income distribution of each socio-economic group was amalgamated into the national income distribution by taking the population shares of the four socio-economic groups as weights[4] (see table 23.3, unadjusted income distributions).

Table 23.3: The distribution of household available income (in percentages); original data and data adjusted for National Accounts, Zambia, 1976

Deciles	Urban areas		Rural areas		Total country	
	Original data	Adjusted	Original data	Adjusted	Original data	Adjusted
I	1.9	1.1	1.2	1.4	1.0	1.0
II	2.7	2.4	2.8	3.3	2.7	2.4
III	3.8	3.3	3.9	4.7	3.0	2.9
IV	4.3	3.7	4.2	5.0	4.5	4.5
V	5.2	4.7	6.8	8.0	5.5	5.2
VI	7.0	5.2	7.7	9.0	6.7	6.0
VII	8.3	7.0	9.6	9.1	8.8	7.6
VIII	11.1	7.8	13.1	12.2	11.2	9.3
IX	18.9	14.9	16.6	15.5	18.2	14.8
X	37.0	50.0	34.1	31.8	38.5	46.3
Gini index	0.48	0.56	0.46	0.41	0.51	0.56

Since the available tabulations for each socio-economic group do not show the structure of income sources for each income class, it was necessary to resort to a somewhat crude adjustment procedure. For each income source, the first step consists in distributing under-reported income between the four socio-economic groups (see table 23.2) and the second step in distributing the under-reported income for each socio-economic group over the income classes. The under-reported wage income is distributed according to the wage shares of each group and among the income classes within each group in proportion with household income as measured by the survey. The under-reported operating surplus is allocated only to the urban households living in high-cost housing areas (9 per cent of total urban households) and distributed in proportion to measured household income. The under-recorded imputed value of own consumption is distributed to the six lowest deciles of the rural income distribution. Table 23.3 shows the results.

4. Conclusion

Adjusting the incomes in urban and rural areas in a dual economy like Zambia has given us also some of the salient features of inequality in such an economy. First, it is normal to expect that the inequality of adjusted income is higher in urban areas and in the country as a whole. The main cause of this is the under-reporting or the non-reporting of various sources of income (especially profits) in the higher income strata.[5] Second, for rural areas a more equal distribution of income was found after adjustment. This may seem odd at first sight, but it should be remembered that the major component of adjustment here was not in the form of unreported wage or profit income but of unreported income in kind (consumption of own produce). Poorer families "spend" usually more on consumption of own produce than richer families.[6] Hence an adjustment for under-reported income in kind will increase the income of the poorer families more than the richer families.

Notes

[1] ILO/UNDP: Second report to the Government of Zambia on incomes, wages and prices in Zambia (Geneva, 1978).

[2] No information is available on the household size of the various income classes. The only information available is the average household size as well as the number of dependants for the various strata in urban areas. The squatter and low-cost housing areas and the high-cost areas show a different picture. In the former, the household size is larger and the number of dependants per worker is almost double. Thus the personal distribution of income in urban areas is more askew than the distribution of household income.

3 Preliminary results are published in Central Statistical Office: Monthly digest of statistics, various issues.

4 Another method of amalgamating distribution figures for different groups is to estimate for each group a continuous distribution and then to construct the joint distribution. It was assumed that household income is log-normally distributed and based upon the gini ratio and the average per head income. This information then permits the calculation of the first two moments (the mean and the variance) of the log-normal distribution. In the case of urban income and national income two different estimates of the variance of the distribution were generated, namely that directly stemming from the decile distribution and that which could be calculated at the moments of a joint distribution (for urban areas consisting of the squatter, low-cost housing and high-cost housing areas and for total Zambia consisting of urban and rural areas). The joint distribution of the urban areas has almost the same gini ratio as those of the distribution derived from an amalgamation of the original tabulations (0.469 compared to 0.479). For the country as a whole, however, the gini indices differ. The joint distribution implies a gini index of 0.543, while that of the amalgamated distribution is 0.513. For more details see also the chapter on Kenya.

5 This is further discussed (also for 1974 figures) in R. van der Hoeven: Income distribution in Zambia, Technical Paper No. 2 in ILO/JASPA: Basic needs in an economy under pressure: Findings and recommendations of an ILO/JASPA basic needs mission to Zambia (Addis Ababa, 1981).

6 idem: Zambia's income inequality during the early seventies (Geneva, ILO, 1977; mimeographed World Employment Programme research working paper; restricted).

ANNEX

COMPARABLE INCOME DISTRIBUTION ESTIMATES
FOR OTHER COUNTRIES

There are various income distribution estimates that are comparable with those provided in this monograph. The main point about the income distribution estimates shown in table A.1 is that the original data have been (fully or partially) adjusted for National Accounts and that the income concept is similar to what was used in this monograph, i.e. household available income. Most estimates were carried out by World Bank collaborators.

Table A.1: Distribution of adjusted household income by households (in percentages).

(The income concept is close to household available income.)

Deciles (households)	Argentina[1] (1970)	Brazil[2] (1972)	Chile[1] (1968)	Costa Rica[1] (1971)	Honduras[2] (1967)	Korea (Rep. of)[3] (1976)	Peru[1] (1972)	Sri Lanka[4] (1969-70)	Venezuela[1] (1970)	United States[5] (1971)
I	1.5	0.6	1.5	0.9	0.7	1.8	0.7	3.1	1.0	1.6
II	2.9	1.4	2.9	2.4	1.6	3.9	1.2	4.4	2.0	3.4
III	4.3	2.1	3.9	3.7	2.2	5.0	1.9	5.4	3.1	4.7
IV	5.4	2.9	5.1	5.0	2.8	6.2	3.2	6.3	4.2	6.1
V	6.3	4.0	6.2	6.1	3.5	7.1	4.6	7.3	5.6	7.5
VI	7.8	5.4	7.6	7.2	4.5	8.3	6.4	8.4	7.3	8.9
VII	10.3	7.1	9.5	8.8	6.4	9.9	8.9	9.8	9.8	10.6
VIII	11.2	9.9	11.9	11.1	10.5	12.5	12.1	11.9	13.0	12.6
IX	15.1	16.0	16.6	15.3	17.8	17.8	18.1	15.1	18.3	15.6
X	35.2	50.6	34.8	39.5	50.0	27.5	43.9	28.3	35.7	29.0
Gini index	0.44	0.61	0.45	0.49	0.61	0.38	0.57	0.35	0.49	0.39

1 Internal World Bank estimates made by Ahlurvalia.

2 Internal World Bank estimates made by Altimir.

3 H. Choo and D. Kim: Probable size distribution of income in Korea: Over time and by sectors (Seoul, Korean Development Institute, 1978; mimeographed).

4 P. Visaria: Poverty and living standards in Asia: An overview of the main results and lessons of selected household surveys (Washington, DC, World Bank, 1980; LSMS working paper No. 2), table 5, p. 184.

5 D.B. Radner and J.C. Hinricks: "Size distribution of income - 1964, 1970, 1971", in Survey of Current Business (Washington, DC, United States Department of Commerce), Oct. 1974, pp. 19-31.